GEOGRAPHY FACTS

GEOGRAPHY FACTS

DOUGAL DIXON

BARNES
&NOBLE
BOOKS
NEW YORK

A QUARTO BOOK

This edition published by
Marboro Books Corp.,
a division of Barnes & Noble Inc.

Copyright © 1992 Quarto Publishing plc

ISBN 0-88029-925-8

This book was designed and produced by
Quarto Publishing plc
The Old Brewery, 6 Blundell Street, London N7 9BH

Senior editor Sally MacEachern
Editor Emma Callery
Art editor Philip Gilderdale
Designer Hugh Schermuly
Illustrators Peter Dennis, Rob Shone, David Kemp
Maps David Kemp
Picture research Rebecca Horsewood
Art director Moira Clinch
Publishing director Janet Slingsby

Typeset in Britain by Brightside Partnership, London
Manufactured in Singapore by J. Film Process Singapore Pte Ltd
Printed in Hong Kong by Leefung-Asco Ltd

CONTENTS

THE STORY OF OUR PLANET

WORLD GAZETTEER

How Did the Earth Begin?

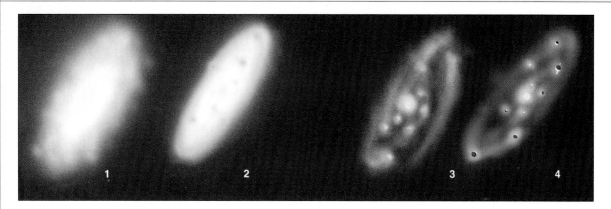

GEOGRAPHY IS THE study of the Earth — the shape and surface of the Earth; why there is land in one place and sea in another; why there are mountains here and plains there; why some areas are lush tropical forest while others are cold desert, and what makes rivers and glaciers flow. It is also the study of how the various peoples of the world fit into all this, choosing to live in one area and not another. But to understand today's world it is necessary to look back in time to discover how the Earth was formed — a story that goes back over six billion years.

1 Back in the mists of time – over 6 billion years ago – the solar system was nothing but a cold cloud of gas and dust floating in space.
2 For some reason – probably to do with the gravitational effects of other masses of material in space – this cloud began to spin. As it did so, it began to flatten out into a disk shape.
3 The bulk of the gas and dust concentrated at the center and began to heat up. Then the ancestral sun formed, and it began to radiate energy to the rest of the solar system.
4 The disk of material around the embryo sun began to split up into rings, and the matter of the rings accumulated into lumps. These were to form the planets, and the other solar system bodies.

IN THE BEGINNING

The current theory of how the Earth and the rest of the solar system formed is that it originated as a cloud of cold dust and gas in space. Even now, such clouds — called nebulae — can be seen through astronomical telescopes. At first, gravitational attraction caused the particles of nebulae to clump together and form a mass at the center. As the cloud

A GOOD ESTIMATE FOR THE TIME

The Earth began at 9:00 AM on October 23 4004BC. These were the findings of Archbishop James Ussher (1581-1656), Archbishop of Armagh from 1625, who worked back from the dates in the Bible to find the actual time of the Creation as described in the Book of Genesis. This figure was inserted as a footnote in the Authorized Version of the Bible until the nineteenth century.

contracted, it began to spin, and the centrifugal action flung much of it out into a disk. Eddies and points of turbulence across this disk produced centers around which the remainder of the cloudy material began to condense. The main mass at the center became the sun, while the material accumulating at these eddies became the planets.

A GRADUAL ACCRETION

The mass that was to become the Earth then became sorted out into its various layers. The heaviest particles, those of iron and nickel, sank to the center while the lighter material, the silicate minerals that produce stony substances, scattered more widely. The force of the gravitational attraction drawing the material together generated a great deal of heat and the interior of the new Earth melted, fused, and distilled. Gases were given off

1 2 3 4   5   6   7

and burst through to the surface where they formed an embryo atmosphere above the hot solid surface. Much of this gas was water vapor and, as soon as the surface of the planet cooled sufficiently, it began to condense, to fall as rain, and to gather in the hollows of the parched landscape. The first oceans began to form.

The mixture of gases left in the atmosphere was quite unlike the air that we breathe today. This first atmosphere consisted mostly of nitrogen and hydrogen. It was not until life evolved in the warm waters that the biochemical processes began that would eventually transform the atmosphere into the mixture with which we are now familiar – a mixture that can support the higher forms of life.

THE EARTH IN MOTION

The spin of the original eddy that produced the Earth is still with us, and even now the planet spins on its axis. It spins once every 24 hours, so maintaining the succession of day and night. Even the spin of the original nebula is still happening. All the planets move around the sun in their orbits, the time taken for each planet to circle the sun being that planet's year. In Earth's case, the year is 365¼ days long.

The axis on which the Earth spins is tilted, in relation to the plane of the orbit. As a result, the North Pole points away from the sun at one part of the orbit and toward the sun at another. This gives us our annual seasons.

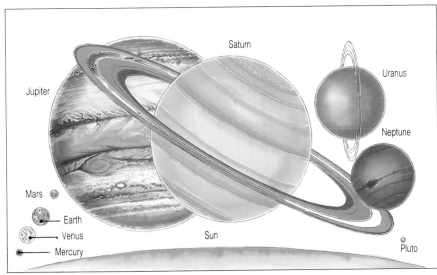

Above When seen from space, the Earth differs obviously from all other planets. The continents and oceans are quite distinct, and the moisture in the atmosphere gives the planet a blue tinge.
Left The planets are either small rocky types – Mercury **1**, Venus **2**, Earth **3**, Mars **4**, and distant Pluto **9** – or huge gassy giants – Jupiter **5**, Saturn **6**, Uranus **7**, and Neptune **8**.
Below With their orbits shown to scale, it can be seen that with the exception of Pluto the small rocky planets orbit close to the sun, while the gas giants are well spread out.

WHAT IS INSIDE THE EARTH?

AS FAR AS we can tell, the Earth is made up of layers, like the layers of an onion. At the center is the core, which is divided into two parts. The inner core is made of iron, heated to such a high temperature and subjected to such a great pressure that we cannot imagine its nature. The rules of conventional physics just do not apply to the Earth's core. The most that can be said is that it is probably solid. Surrounding the inner core is the outer core, also made of iron, which seems to be liquid.

The central core is shrouded by the mantle, a layer that makes up most of the Earth's bulk. It consists of stony materials and is solid, although there is a soft layer toward the surface.

On the surface there is the crust which is the thinnest of rinds on the outside, and of which there are two types. The oceanic crust is fairly dense and underlies the oceans. It is made up predominantly of silica and magnesium, a substance that the geophysicists call SIMA. The continental crust is much more complex and the rocks are made of a lighter substance. The main components are silica and aluminum — the geophysicists call it SIAL. The continental crust is formed as separate blocks embedded in the oceanic crust. Finally, there is the watery layer forming the oceans, and the gassy layer forming the atmosphere.

A GLOBE?

Although the world is described as being round, its sphericity is, in fact, slightly blemished. Apart from the topographical irregularities — the mountain peaks and the ocean troughs — there is a distinct flattening at each pole, formed by the spin of the Earth on its axis. The equatorial diameter is 7,926 miles (12,756km) while the polar diameter is only 7,900 miles (12,713km), a difference of 26 miles (43km).

HOW DO WE KNOW?

We opened this page with "As far as we can tell..." because no one has actually seen inside the Earth. The deepest hole is in the Kola Peninsula of Russia — a borehole that reached a depth of 40,226 feet (12,261m) in 1991. This was only about a tenth of the way through the Earth's crust, and they were still drilling.

Earthquakes can help us to understand what is inside the Earth. When an earthquake occurs it sets up vibrations through the substance of the Earth, and these vibrations travel as shock

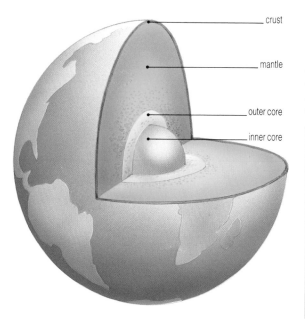

crust

mantle

outer core

inner core

Left At the center of the Earth is the inner core which is a solid mass of compressed iron. This is surrounded by the outer core, a liquid form of the same material. Then comes the stony mantle and finally the crust. The two types of crust form the thinnest of skins.

Below Human attempts to pierce the crust of the Earth are feeble. The greatest mining feats can only scratch the surface. Kimberley Big Hole, a disused diamond mine in South Africa, is grand in human terms, but at 1,000ft (300m) it hardly penetrates the surface.

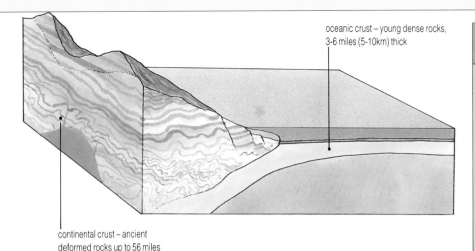

oceanic crust – young dense rocks, 3-6 miles (5-10km) thick

continental crust – ancient deformed rocks up to 56 miles (90km) thick

MOHO MAKES HIS NAME

Andrija Mohorovicic (1857-1936) was a meteorologist working in what was then the Austro-Hungarian Empire. He established a seismological observatory after an earthquake struck Zagreb in 1901. In 1909, he analyzed the shock waves generated by another earthquake in the Kulpa valley and from them he determined that there was a marked boundary between the crust and the mantle. This boundary is now called the Mohorovicic discontinuity, or the Moho for short.

waves. There are two main types of wave — the "P" wave that is compressional, and the "S" wave that has a shaking effect. "P" waves can pass through solids and liquids, while "S" waves can only pass through solids. The patterns of waves detected at the far side of the Earth from a particular earthquake can indicate the kinds of materials through which they passed. Also, earthquake waves are refracted, or bent, as they pass through materials of different densities. This again affects the pattern on the Earth's surface, and can be used to study the nature of the deep materials.

Above There are two types of crust. The oceanic crust is made of dense material called SIMA, consisting of rocks composed of minerals rich in silica and magnesium. The material of the continental crust – SIAL – is much lighter, consisting of all kinds of rocks in which silica and aluminum are important. Continental crust comes in separate lumps, made up of twisted and contorted rocks, and it is embedded in the oceanic crust which is structurally quite simple and fairly young.

Below The Earth's magnetic field can be felt well out into space. The field reacts with the stream of charged particles from the sun, which pulls it out into an elongated teardrop shape.

A BIG MAGNET

The solid inner core, being separated from the rest of the Earth by the liquid outer core, is free to spin at a different rate from the rest of the planet. As a result a magnetic field is generated. The physics involved are similar to those that involve magnetism in the turning of an electric motor or a dynamo. In effect, the whole Earth acts as a giant magnet, with its poles close to the North and South geographic poles. The magnetic field generated can be detected over the whole of the Earth and is used as a navigation aid — compasses always point to the north magnetic pole. Migrating birds and fishes can also detect the field and use it in their migrations.

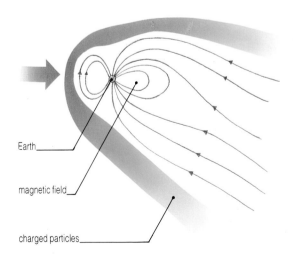

Earth

magnetic field

charged particles

WHAT WAS EARTH'S EARLY HISTORY?

THE OLDEST KNOWN rock lies in Greenland. It is part of a sequence of rocks that is 3.8 billion years old. On the face of it this may seem a long time ago but as the Earth is some 4.5 billion years old, this rock was formed quite a way into the story. The ancient rocks in Greenland are examples of gneissic rock and are metamorphic — that is, they were formed as heat and pressure changed a rock that was already in existence. Previously this rock would have been a sedimentary rock, like sandstone, made up of tiny grains and fragments. These fragments would, in turn, have been worn off some other rock that existed even before this. Earth history is extremely complex!

Some of the most ancient rocks are sedimentary and have not been metamorphosed. These are known as greenstones and are interesting because they contain iron ore that has not been combined with oxygen, suggesting that there was no free oxygen in the atmosphere at that time. Iron ores that form nowadays tend to be reddish in color as they are combined with oxygen. We are familiar with this effect in the rusting of exposed iron. The red substance known as rust is an oxide of iron.

LIFE EVOLVES

At around 3.8 billion years ago life began. The earliest form of life occurred in the sea and was probably no more than a molecule that had the power to reproduce itself by absorbing the chemicals present in the water. Any change to the molecule that made reproduction more efficient would have been passed on to the offspring molecules, and so evolution would have begun. The first living cells were probably cyanobacteria — sometimes called "blue-green algae" — similar to those that can form a poisonous scum on modern bodies of water. Microscopic organisms like these leave no fossils but they can leave signs of their passing. Where mats of cyanobacteria lie on the seabed, the currents bring sand particles that become entangled with the organisms. A new mat of bacteria will form on the sand layer, which will in turn attract more sand. The result is a dome-like structure, called a stromatolite, consisting of alternating sand and bacteria layers. Such structures can only form in waters where there are no other living things to disturb them, and they

Left The oldest rocks of the world lie at the cores of the continents. These consist of metamorphic rocks – rocks that have been formed from pre-existing rocks. They have been twisted, deformed and compressed so much that they cannot fold any more, and have been worn flat by billions of years of continual erosion. Such areas are called "shields" and are found at the hearts of all the continents. So compact are they that mountain-building processes cannot affect them, and any new mountains in the area are thrust up from the younger sedimentary and surrounding igneous rocks. A typical continent will have a central shield surrounded by younger mountain ranges. The photograph shows what a section of the Canadian Shield looks like from the air.

Continental shields

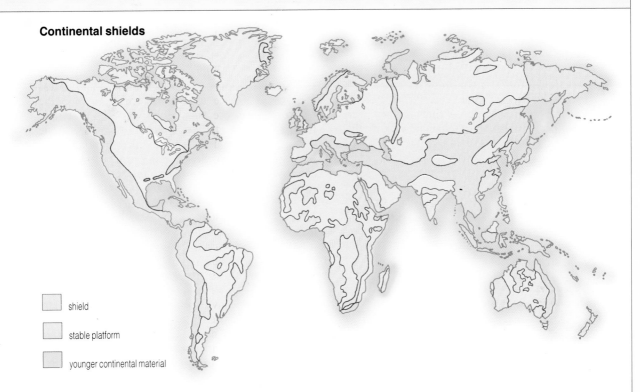

☐ shield

☐ stable platform

☐ younger continental material

were much more common in ancient times than in modern waters. They have been found in rocks 3.5 billion years old.

Some primitive microorganisms powered their reproductive cycle by absorbing energy from the sun. We can think of these as the first plants. Other organisms did not use the raw chemical materials but absorbed the ready-made foodstuffs and molecules produced by the early plants. These were the first animals. The chemical process that uses the sun's energy for reproduction produces oxygen as a by-product, and this was given off and dissolved in the ocean waters or put into the atmosphere. Free oxygen – oxygen gas that is not combined with any other substance — was present in the atmosphere by 2 billion years ago.

Above The exposed shields lie in the hearts of the continents. Those in the east of South America were once continuous with those in the west of Africa, but the two continents have since split apart. Sometimes the shields are covered by later, undisturbed sedimentary rock, in which case they are called "stable platforms." The younger portions of the continents, formed by mountain-chains, surround the shield.

LIFE-GIVING AIR?

If we had been in existence 2 billion years ago we would have been poisoned by our own atmosphere. It was only after plant life evolved that free oxygen was generated.

THE GROWTH OF CONTINENTS

While all this was happening in the sea, what was happening on the land? As well as the metamorphic rocks which formed the cores of the continents, and the sedimentary rocks in the surrounding seas, there is a third type of rock which was produced by volcanic action. This is called igneous rock and was created when molten rock solidified. The continents grew from their metamorphic cores as mountain-building processes along the edges threw up chains of sedimentary rock, shot through by igneous rock. Nowadays, most continents consist of a core of ancient metamorphic rock surrounded by successively younger suites of sedimentary and igneous rocks in the form of mountains.

HOW IS EARTH TIME MEASURED?

EON	ERA	PERIOD	EPOCH	AGE
PHANEROZOIC	CENOZOIC	Quaternary	Holocene	0.01
			Pleistocene	1.64
		Tertiary	Pliocene	
			Miocene	
			Oligocene	
			Eocene	
			Paleocene	65
	MESOZOIC	Cretaceous		146
		Jurassic		208
		Triassic		245
	PALEOZOIC — Late	Permian		290
		Pennsylvanian		323
		Mississippian		363
	PALEOZOIC — Early	Devonian		409
		Silurian		439
		Ordovician		510
		Cambrian		570
PROTEROZOIC	LATE PRECAMBRIAN			
ARCHAEAN	EARLY PRECAMBRIAN			

JUST AS WE divide human history into periods according to the events or the rulers of the time — pre-Columbian, Ming, Victorian, and so on, so we divide the vast sweep of geological time into periods and eras based on the kinds of animals and plants that existed during those times.

For about seven-eighths of the time that the Earth has been in existence, what life there was left little in the way of fossils. For this reason, this vast period, called the Precambrian era, tends to be dismissed. It is divided into two eons: the Archaean, in which there was no life, and the Peroterozoic, in which life of some sort existed.

Then, 570 million years ago, the Paleozoic era began. This opened with the Cambrian in which there was a sudden flourishing of animals with hard shells. From then onward, the rocks are full of fossils. The Lower Paleozoic, consisting of the Cambrian, Ordovician and Silurian periods, showed a great development of life in the sea and the evolution of the first backboned animals — the fish. In the Upper Paleozoic — the Devonian, Carboniferous and Permian periods — life colonized the land. Plants left the water first, followed by invertebrates that developed into insects and spiders, then came the amphibians and these evolved into reptiles.

During the Mesozoic era — consisting of the Triassic, Jurassic, and Cretaceous periods — the pattern of life changed. At the beginning, the primitive reptiles evolved into the dinosaurs, that

THE NAMES OF THE AGES

The names of the geological periods are mostly taken from the areas where their rocks were studied.
● Quarternary and Tertiary: these names are throwbacks to an early classification that divided geological time into four parts.
● Cretaceous: after the Latin for chalk.
● Jurassic: after the Jura mountains in Germany.
● Triassic: after the threefold division of the rocks, as found in Germany.
● Permian: after Perm in Russia.
● Carboniferous: after the carbon from the coal deposits.
● Pennsylvanian: after Pennsylvania.
● Mississippian: after Mississippi.
● Devonian: after Devon in southwestern England.
● Silurian and Ordovician: after ancient Welsh tribes.
● Cambrian: after the old name for Wales.

Below (inset) Fossils are a geologist's most important timekeepers. Over the last two centuries of geological exploration fossils from all over the world have been collected and compared. The longevity of many of the extinct creatures has been determined and so the dates of the most common fossils are well known and documented. If one of these fossils is found in a rock then that rock must have formed during the time that the creature is known to have existed. If several recognizable fossils are found then the rock was formed during the time in which the lifespans of these species overlapped.

Right In an unconformity one set of rocks is overlain by another. In this example the lower beds have been tilted and eroded flat and then the upper beds laid down on them. The upper beds must be much younger than the lower.

dominated the land throughout the era, and into the mammals, that were to play a less prominent role for a while. In the sea, too, changes were taking place, with modern-type fish evolving.

A sudden mass extinction brought the Mesozoic to an end — an extinction that saw the loss of the dinosaurs and many of the sea creatures. The Cenozoic era then began, and in this time the mammals radiated to fill all the niches left vacant by the extinction of the great reptiles. The bulk of the Cenozoic is taken up by the Tertiary period. The last sliver is known as the Quaternary period and this embraces the Ice Age and modern times in which human beings developed.

The rocks that were laid down in these various periods can usually be dated by the types of fossils found in them. That is fine when we are dealing with sedimentary rocks in which fossils are abundant, but what about metamorphic rocks and igneous rocks, or even unfossiliferous sedimentary rocks? Here the principle of crosscutting relationships is used. If a metamorphic rock has been formed by the alteration of a sedimentary rock containing Silurian fossils, then the metamorphism must have taken place after the Silurian period. If this metamorphic rock is cut across by a crack filled with igneous rock, then the igneous rock must have been formed later still. If this whole sequence is then overlain by undisturbed sedimentary rock containing Carboniferous fossils, then we can deduce

that the metamorphism and the igneous emplacement took place between Silurian and Carboniferous times, in the Devonian period.

HOW DO WE PUT DATES TO ALL THIS?

We can glibly talk about the hundreds of millions of years involved in the geological time scale, but how is such a scale calibrated? The secret lies in the radioactive elements in the Earth's crust. A radioactive element will decay to a non-radioactive form in a specific length of time. For example, after a mineral containing potassium-40 is formed it will take a known length of time for half the mass of potassium-40 to decay into argon-40, then the same period of time for half of the remainder to decay, and so on. This period is known as the "half-life." By finding the proportion of potassium-40 to argon-40 in a mineral we can work out how long ago that mineral formed. Many radioactive elements are used, each with a different half-life.

HOW HAS ANIMAL LIFE CHANGED?

MOST PEOPLE, WHEN asked what life was like in the past, will immediately think of dinosaurs, or of coal forests, or of early humans. These things did exist, but only as part of a complex pattern and sequence of events. The animal and plant life that we see around us now represents only a snapshot, an instantaneous glimpse, of this whole changing panoply. The animal life will be as different in five million years' time as it was five million years ago.

Evolution is the term that we use when talking about the changing nature of life on Earth. It is the process that developed living things from reproducing molecules, to single-celled animals, to multi-celled organisms, to worms, to fish, to amphibians, to reptiles, to mammals, and has culminated in ourselves. Yet this is an over-simplistic view — a view that has come about because we think of ourselves as the dominant species in the world today — the pinnacle of evolution. The true process is much more complex.

BUST, THEN BOOM

Extinction — a term that strikes horror and shame into the hearts of those who love the wildlife of our planet — has an indispensable role in the process of evolution. Each creature occupies its own ecological niche, that is the way of life within a particular environment. It is a rule of nature that once an ecological niche becomes vacant — if its occupant becomes extinct — something will evolve to fill it. This is complicated by the fact that creatures often become extinct because the environment changes. In which case the resulting ecological niche will be somewhat different from the one that went before, but still something will evolve to fill it.

Time and again in the geological record we see mass extinctions, when whole groups of creatures die out at once, immediately followed by a sudden expansion and diversification of those that are left. At the beginning of the Cambrian period hard-shelled animals suddenly appeared. These immediately diverged into all kinds of weird and wonderful shapes to occupy the ecological niches that existed at the time. It is as if nature were trying out all sorts of animal designs to see what worked. After a few million years, the vast majority of these creatures had died out, leaving a few successful lines that developed into the subsequent fauna of the Earth. The same thing happened at the end of the Cretaceous period when all the dinosaurs and the specialized flying and swimming reptiles died out. The mammals survived and spread out to fill the niches that had been occupied by the reptiles. Again a vast number of very strange creatures appeared, which was soon whittled down to the few groups that eventually evolved into the mammal life that we know today.

AN IDEA FOR ITS TIME

Charles Darwin (1809-82) was not the first scientist who had theorized on evolution. The idea had been around for centuries. However, he was the first who, through the concept of natural selection, proposed a workable mechanism for it. At the same time, the naturalist Alfred Russel Wallace (1823-1913) came up with essentially the same idea.

Below Fossils of extinct animals, such as these ammonites – shelled relatives of the octopus and squid – tell us how life has changed throughout the history of our planet.

GEOGRAPHY OF THE PAST

By these processes the continents were populated and the seas were filled with animals. The fossils left behind by these creatures in the sedimentary rocks formed at that time show us how different were the geographical conditions in the past. Deep sea fossils in the highest parts of the Rockies show where once there had been deep seas. Dinosaur footprints in Spitzbergen show that climates within the modern Arctic Circle must have been quite different from now. Fossils of the same land animals in South America and Africa show that once the Atlantic Ocean did not exist and the animals could move freely from one area to another.

Bottom A glimpse of modern wildlife, such as this scene of an elephant grazing in Africa's Great Rift valley, is merely a passing moment in the shifting pattern of life's history.

Below Fossils of tropical plants found in modern polar latitudes show how the environment has changed through time.

HAVE THE CONTINENTS MOVED?

TAKE A LOOK at a map of the world. Has it ever struck you that the west coast of Africa looks suspiciously like the east coast of South America – like the adjacent pieces of a jigsaw puzzle? It is a similarity that has struck many people ever since maps became accurate enough to show it.

The implication behind this is that the continents were not always distributed as they are today, but have been moved across the Earth's surface at some time in the past. Only with the publication of the book *The Origin of Continents and Oceans* by Alfred Wegener in 1915 did the idea come to merit scientific consideration. The process was dubbed "continental drift," but it was not until the 1960s that anybody had any idea about the mechanism.

Surveys of the ocean floors showed that they were spreading. Through all the oceans of the world there is a series of ridges. Along these ridges molten material is welling up from inside the Earth and solidifying. New ocean floor material is continually being emplaced at the ridge crest, which is then split and moved apart as more floor material is emplaced in the cracks. In this continuous process the ocean floor at each side of an ocean ridge is moving away from the ridge, like a conveyor belt.

THE PROOF?

At the crest of a ridge, the fresh material is erupted from underwater volcanoes. These form lava structures called pillow lavas on the ocean floor. A mile or two from a ridge, these pillow lavas have a sprinkling of sediment upon them. A few miles further on they are buried in sediment, showing that the ocean floor is older further from a ridge crest, having existed for long enough to gather a layer of sediment, like dust in a neglected room.

It has also been found that as a rock forms the magnetic minerals in it align themselves with the Earth's magnetic field. We know that the magnetic field reverses itself, north for south, every few thousand years. The rocks at a ridge crest are magnetized according to the modern polarity of the field, but not far away they will have a reversed polarity, as if they were formed at a time when the polarity of the Earth was reversed. Further away they will show the normal polarity again.

A WIDENING OCEAN

The Atlantic ocean is 33ft (10m) wider now than it was when Christopher Columbus crossed it in 1492.

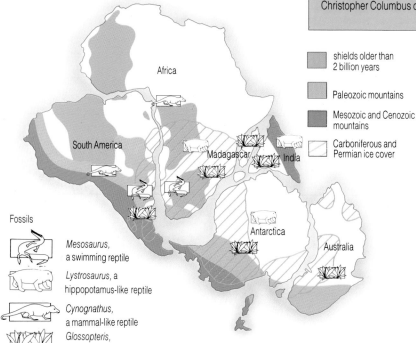

Fossils

Mesosaurus, a swimming reptile

Lystrosaurus, a hippopotamus-like reptile

Cynognathus, a mammal-like reptile

Glossopteris, a seed fern

shields older than 2 billion years

Paleozoic mountains

Mesozoic and Cenozoic mountains

Carboniferous and Permian ice cover

Left For a large period of Earth's history all the southern continents were joined together as one continuous landmass that we now call Gondwana. There are several pieces of evidence for this. As well as the fit of the coastlines, there are ancient mountain ranges that would be continuous if the continents were reassembled in their former position. Also, an ice age of about 300 million years ago has left its mark, showing the former presence of a continuous ice cover over part of the combined continents. Fossils of the same animals and plants are widespread. Gondwana finally broke up about 50 million years ago.

Below When Gondwana broke up, first South America split away from Africa during the Jurassic period, and India and Madagascar from Africa during the Cretaceous period. Australia did not split from Antarctica until the Tertiary. India has since collided with Asia.

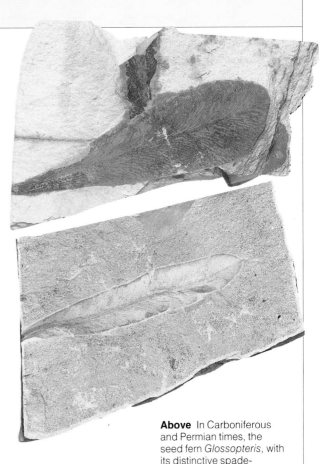

Above In Carboniferous and Permian times, the seed fern *Glossopteris*, with its distinctive spade-shaped leaves, was a common plant throughout the southern hemisphere. Its fossils have been found on all the southern continents.

THE INFERENCE?

When the evidence is put together we find that the outer surface of the Earth is constantly on the move. It is made up of separate panels, or plates, like the panels of a soccer ball. Each plate consists of the crust and the topmost layer of the mantle, and it moves on the soft layer of mantle that exists not far from the surface. Each plate is growing along one seam, which is represented by the ocean ridges. But simultaneously, each is being destroyed at the other seam. At the deep ocean troughs, one plate is sliding down and is being swallowed up beneath the other. The mass of continental crust is lighter than the oceanic crust and it is carried around, embedded in the plates like logs embedded in a frozen river. Such is the explanation of the movement of continents. The whole concept is generally known as "plate tectonics."

THE SHATTERED ZOO

About 300 million years ago, during the Triassic period, the southern part of Pangaea was clothed in a vegetation consisting mostly of the fern *Glossopteris*. A hippopotamus-like reptile called *Lystrosaurus* lived there, hunted by a wolf-like reptile *Cynognathus*. In the lakes lived the swimming reptile *Mesosaurus*. Nowadays, fossils of *Mesosaurus* are found in Brazil and South Africa, those of *Lystrosaurus* in South Africa, India and Antarctica, those of *Cynognathus* in Africa and India, and those of *Glossopteris* are scattered across South America, Africa, India, Antarctica, and Australia.

How Have the Continents Moved?

Below The surface of our planet is on the move, with the ocean floor constantly being created, then shifting and being destroyed, with the continents being moved along in the process. The surface plates of the Earth are formed from the crust and part of the mantle. New plate material, consisting of ocean crust and topmost mantle, is being created at the ocean ridges. The ocean floor therefore continues to move. When the edge of one plate meets another, one plate sinks beneath the other forming an ocean trough. Where a plate sinks beneath a continent there are coastal mountain ranges and volcanoes.

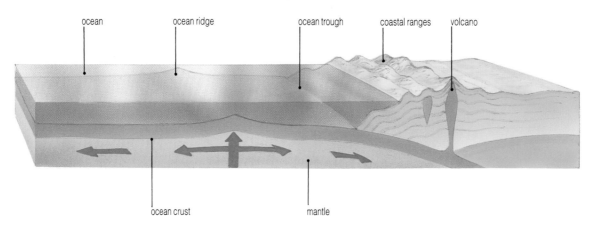

BECAUSE OF PLATE tectonics we now know that the geography of our planet has had as spectacular an evolutionary history as has the animal and plant life of our planet. The moving plates have carried the continents about, smashed them into one another, and torn them apart.

The earliest continents would have consisted of blocks of igneous or metamorphic rocks, embedded in oceanic crust. The ocean floors would have had ocean ridges, where the new plate material was being generated, and ocean troughs where it was being destroyed. As one ocean plate was being drawn down, or subducted, beneath another the continent embedded in it moved toward the ocean trough. When it reached the trough the whole system jammed, since the continental SIAL would have been too light to be drawn down. Eventually, the process would have begun again, but this time with the other ocean plate being drawn down under the edge of the continent. This would have caused the sediments at the edge of the continent to be crumpled up forming mountain ranges of sedimentary rocks along the continent's edge. These rocks would have been shot through with igneous rocks, which were formed as the subducting plate melted at depth and the molten material arose through the overlying crust.

Such processes happen at the present day. When the moving plates send one continent crashing into another, the two coastal mountain ranges combine to form one huge mountain range along the joint. When a new constructive plate margin begins beneath a continent, the continent splits open and the two parts move apart, opening a new ocean between them.

MIX 'N' MATCH CONTINENTS

We can follow the movement of continents throughout the geological record. In the early Paleozoic, the continents were quite different from today's and they were scattered across the globe. A significant continental movement at these times was the approach of the continent that was to become North America to that which was to become northern Europe. These two continents collided in Devonian times and the mountains thrown up between them can now be seen as the Scottish and Norwegian Highlands and part of the Appalachians. In the Carboniferous, the northern Europe landmass collided with that of Siberia forming the Urals along the joint. Then Africa met the North-American/European landmass and the remainder of the Appalachians were emplaced.

By Triassic times, all the fragments of continental crust had come together and fused into a single gigantic supercontinent that we now call Pangaea.

There were two parts to this great continent — a northern section called Laurasia and a southern section called Gondwana. Between the two there was a great embayment called the Tethys Sea. The oceans of the world were also united into a single huge ocean, called Panthalassa.

However, Pangaea did not exist for long. In Jurassic times, it began to split apart. The first split formed the northern Atlantic ocean, pulling North America away from Europe. This was followed by the opening of the south Atlantic. India did not break away from the mass of Gondwana until the Cretaceous, after which it crossed the Tethys and collided with Asia, throwing up the Himalayas between

HIDDEN VIOLENCE

The vast proportion of volcanic activity happening today is never seen by human eyes, for it takes place along the crest of the ocean ridges. A recent survey of part of the North Atlantic ridge has shown a count of 481 volcanoes in an area of 2,300 square miles (6,000 km^2).

them. Australia was the last to move, not making the break from Gondwana until early in the Tertiary. It has been moving northward ever since.

Plate margins

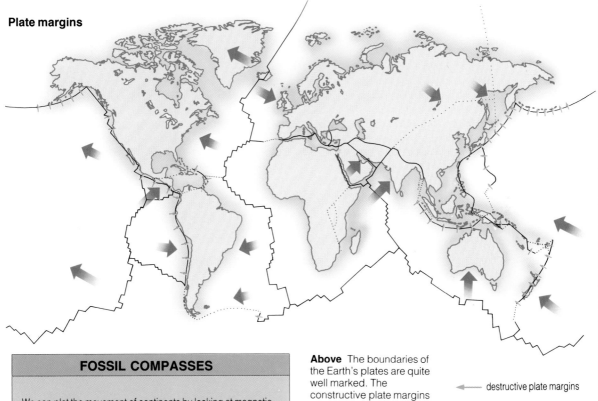

FOSSIL COMPASSES

We can plot the movement of continents by looking at magnetic minerals in rocks. When a rock is emplaced the magnetic field of any magnetic mineral in it will become aligned with the Earth's magnetic pole. This means that the orientation of a mineral's field will tell us the direction of the pole at the time the rock formed.

Above The boundaries of the Earth's plates are quite well marked. The constructive plate margins – where new plates are being created – lie along the ocean ridges. The destructive margins coincide with ocean troughs or with mountain ranges. Volcanoes and earthquakes are frequent along all margins.

⟵ destructive plate margins

◀ direction of plate movement

· · · · · probable plate margins

⌐⌐⌐ constructive plate margins

WHAT IS A VOLCANO?

IF YOU WANT proof that all this plate tectonic activity is still taking place you need look no further than the volcanic areas of the world. Most volcanoes are found along the plate margins where new plate material is being created or old material is being destroyed. As plate creation and plate destruction are two separate processes it is hardly surprising that there are two distinct types of volcano.

NATURE'S FIREWORK DISPLAY

At a constructive plate margin, molten material wells up from the Earth's mantle and injects itself into the crust, solidifying into vertical slabs and building out the new plate material. The molten matter that bursts through to the surface produces volcanoes. This mantle material cools and changes its composition on the way up, but when it erupts, it forms a dark-colored lava that contains relatively little of the mineral silica. Such a lava is quite runny, forming spectacular fountains of glowing liquid and rivers of molten rock. It solidifies to form the rock called basalt.

Usually basaltic lava is erupted at the bottom of the ocean, this being where all plate construction takes place. However, sometimes, as in Iceland, the basalt builds up such a pile that it forms islands. Basalts can also form far from any plate margin. A spot of particularly intense activity in the mantle may send up hot plumes of mantle material that can break through the crust anywhere. The moving plate above such a stationary "hot spot" gives rise to an active volcano and a chain of progressively older

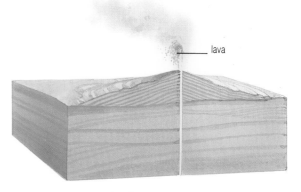

basaltic volcano

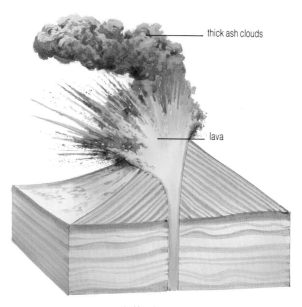

thick ash clouds

lava

andesitic volcano

Left The bubbling, glowing mountains of Hawaii present the popular image of a volcano. However, such volcanoes are only found at constructive plate margins and over "hot spots". On land, the more common type of volcano is the steep-sided type that erupts violently causing a great deal of damage and death.

Above The basaltic volcano is formed from very runny lava erupted gently. It flows some distance before solidifying, and produces a flat shield volcano. Conversely, the thick lava of an andesitic volcano forces its way through the rocks and explodes at the surface, producing thick ash clouds and a towering volcano.

extinct volcanic islands. Hawaii and the Galapagos islands are the classic examples.

Basaltic volcanoes are broad and flat, as the lava tends to run for long distances and spread out before solidifying. As the eruptions are fairly gentle, basaltic volcanoes are tourist attractions.

KILLERS

A quite different kind of volcano lies at the destructive plate margin. As one plate is drawn down beneath another and destroyed, the material of the subducting plate melts, and rises through the edge of the plate above, eventually bursting out at the Earth's surface.

The lava produced by such action, being formed from molten plate material, has a chemical composition that is rich in silica. This makes the lava stiff and easily solidified and produces a rock called andesite. The viscosity of andesitic lava means that it does not flow far before solidifying, and so it builds up steep-sided conical volcanoes. Often the lava solidifies in the volcanic vent, and the build-up of pressure beneath produces a vast explosion and widespread destruction.

Where an oceanic plate is being destroyed beneath another oceanic plate, these volcanoes show themselves as an arc of volcanic islands, such as those that festoon the western part of the Pacific Ocean. Mount Pinatubo in the Philippines is a spectacular example. But where an oceanic plate is being destroyed beneath a continental plate, the volcanoes are thrust up through the mountain chain forming at the continent's edge. This is happening along the length of the Andes — hence the name of the lava — and the coast ranges of North America. Mount Saint Helens was the famous example of the 1980s. No tourist attractions these, andesitic volcanoes are treated with fear and respect.

TWO FAMOUS ERUPTIONS

● One of the most famous historical eruptions was that of Vesuvius in AD 79 in which a blast of ash killed 20,000 inhabitants of nearby Pompeii. It is well-known because Pliny the Younger produced a vivid eyewitness account, and painstaking archeological work has been undertaken there.

● Another famous eruption was that of Krakatoa in Indonesia in 1883. Sea waves generated by the blast spread halfway around the world and killed 36,000 people. This is well-known because news of the disaster was quickly spread by the newly installed telegraph system.

Volcano distribution

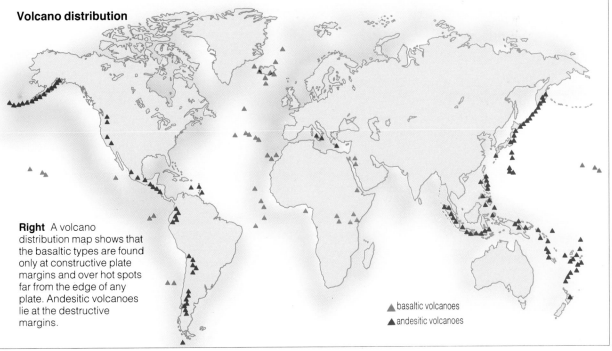

Right A volcano distribution map shows that the basaltic types are found only at constructive plate margins and over hot spots far from the edge of any plate. Andesitic volcanoes lie at the destructive margins.

▲ basaltic volcanoes
▲ andesitic volcanoes

HOW DO EARTHQUAKES OCCUR?

THE MOVEMENTS OF the tectonic plates, their growth and the destruction of one beneath another, do not take place as smooth, well-oiled processes. As one plate jostles against another, the friction builds up tensions as plates are locked together, and these are only released in a sudden burst when the strains are too much for the rocks to bear. The result is an earthquake.

WHERE?

As with the belts of volcanic activity, the earthquake-prone zones tend to coincide with the Earth's plate margins — particularly the destructive plate margins. At a destructive plate margin the earthquakes are quite shallow at the line of surface contact between plates. Away from the surface plate margin the earthquakes become deeper and deeper, corres-

ponding to the depth of the subducting plate. The deepest earthquakes take place at depths of about 375 miles (600km).

The point at which the maximum movement takes place is called the earthquake's focus. The point on the Earth's surface directly above the focus is called the epicenter. Usually most damage occurs at the epicenter, but this can vary with the nature of the ground. The epicenter of the Mexican earthquake of 1985 was near the Pacific coast, but most damage was done in Mexico City 250 miles (400km) away, because the city was built on soft lake deposits that magnified the vibrations.

WHAT HAPPENS IN AN EARTHQUAKE?

As the plates grind by one another they set up tensions in the rocks along the contact. When they finally give way, they do so along a crack called a fault. The rock masses suddenly slip past one another along the fault, creating the shock waves that we feel as the earthquake. The masses move with such force that before they stop they are carried past their point of equilibrium, and so they are still unstable. Over the next few days they tend to shuffle back and forth before they settle down, and it is this movement that produces the aftershocks that so often follow a major earthquake.

HOW IS AN EARTHQUAKE MEASURED?

There are two ways in which we can measure an earthquake. The first is by its intensity, measured on the Mercalli scale. The intensity of a particular earthquake varies from place to place. At the epicenter it may have an intensity of 10 which is enough to produce serious structural damage. A hundred miles (160km) away it may have an intensity of 5 in which minor damage results. A thousand miles (1600km) away it may have an intensity of 1, and only be detected by sensitive instruments.

The other measurement is the magnitude, measured on the Richter scale. This is a function of the total energy released and so a particular earthquake will have only one reading on the Richter scale. The strongest earthquakes are about 8 on this scale. The Richter scale is logarithmic — each point is ten times the value of the point below it. Hence if an earthquake measures 6 on the Richter scale and is

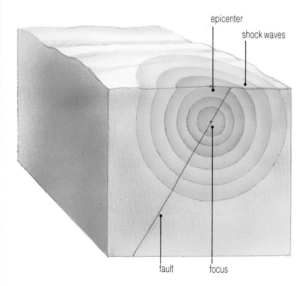

epicenter

shock waves

fault   focus

Above When two masses of rock slide by one another suddenly, the result is an earthquake. The crack along which the masses move is called a fault. The point at which most movement takes place is called the focus. Energy radiates away from the focus as shock waves and the epicenter on the Earth's surface is directly above

the focus. The effect of the earthquake can be felt over a large area, usually diminishing with distance away from the epicenter. The different intensities of the earthquake on the Earth's surface can be plotted using contour lines called isoseisms.

MERCALLI SCALE

1 Only felt by instruments.
2 Felt by people at rest. Hanging objects swing.
3 Felt indoors. Standing cars rock.
4 Sleepers awakened. Windows rattle.
5 Plaster falls. Windows break.
6 Felt by everybody. Chimneys fall.
7 Felt in moving cars. Moderate damage to buildings.
8 Walls and statues fall. People panic.
9 Weak structures totally destroyed. Underground pipes break. Ground cracks.
10 Most buildings destroyed. Railway lines bend.
11 Cracks produce noticeable fault scarps.
12 Objects thrown into the air. Total destruction.

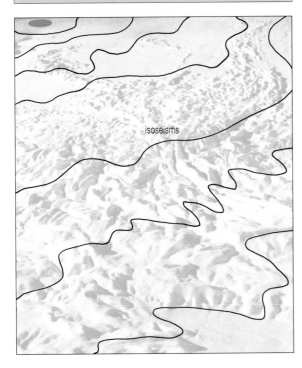

isoseisms

SIDE EFFECTS

When an earthquake occurs offshore, the shock is often transferred to the water above. This can then build up in shallow water and form a destructive wave called a *tsunami*. Or, when an earthquake hits a mountainous area, landslides are a common occurrence because when shaken, loose soil can form a mass that behaves like a fluid.

Left The pattern of isoseisms from an earthquake is broadly concentric but is modified by the geography.

Above Earthquake damage is familiar to anyone who watches news reports. The "X"-shaped and diagonal cracks in this building after an earthquake in Sicily in 1985 are typical of those produced by earthquake vibrations at intensity 7.

BIG EARTHQUAKES

Earthquake	Richter scale value	Number of fatalities
Shansi 1556	Unknown	830,000
Lisbon 1755	8.7	20,000
Naples 1857	6.5	12,000
San Francisco 1906	8.3	700
Alaska 1964	8.6	115
Tangshan 1967	8.2	242,000
Armenia 1988	6.9	25,000
Iran 1991	7.7	50,000

followed by an aftershock of force 5, the aftershock is only a tenth of the strength of the original quake, a point often missed by journalists.

A device called a seismometer is used for the Richter scale measurement. A suspended weight remains stationary by its own inertia, while the observatory shakes around it. The relative movements are amplified by a system of levers and recorded as a wave on a graph.

HOW ARE MOUNTAINS BUILT?

THE MOUNTAINS OF our planet are another result of plate tectonics. Land is continually worn away by the weather and other forms of erosion. The rocks — sedimentary, igneous, or metamorphic — are broken down into fragments and carried out to sea by rivers and wind. There they settle as layers of sediment. Eventually they become sedimentary rock. This change usually takes place at the edge of a continent. If that continent subsequently moves to a destructive plate margin and an adjacent plate begins to subduct beneath it, then the process of mountain-building begins.

FOLDS

As the oceanic plate grinds down beneath the continent, the sedimentary rocks that were forming between them are crushed and faulted, twisted and thrust upward against the continent's edge. A million earthquakes over the millions of years gradually shear the rocks into chunks and fold them into complex shapes. Under great pressures, the layers, or beds, of rock fold like layers of cloth. Folds that sag downward are called synclines. Folds that arch upward are called anticlines. As the mountains rise, the process of erosion continues, wearing them away and exposing the twisted nature of the rocks within them.

The greatest mountain chains in the world are fold mountains such as these. The Andes are the classic example. Running for 5,530 miles (8,850km) down the western coast of South America they represent the longest mountain chain in the world. They are being thrown up as the continent thrusts westward against the Pacific plate which is subducting along the ocean trench that lies just offshore.

Below The relentless force of an ocean plate shoving its way below a continental plate continually crumples up the edge of the continent. The sediments being deposited at the continent's edge, as well as the sediments already converted to sedimentary rocks, are compressed and thrust up into long fold mountain chains.

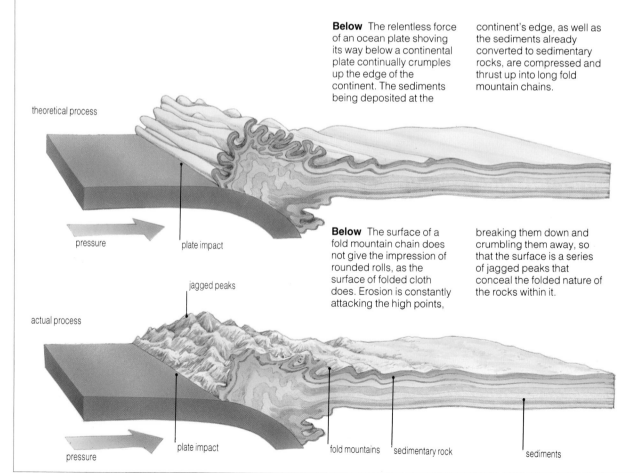

theoretical process

pressure

plate impact

jagged peaks

actual process

pressure

plate impact

fold mountains   sedimentary rock   sediments

Below The surface of a fold mountain chain does not give the impression of rounded rolls, as the surface of folded cloth does. Erosion is constantly attacking the high points, breaking them down and crumbling them away, so that the surface is a series of jagged peaks that conceal the folded nature of the rocks within it.

Left The highest mountains are the youngest. The Himalayas and Karakorams only started rising some 50 million years ago. India at this time had broken away from Antarctica, where it had formed part of the supercontinent Gondwana, and was approaching the continent of Asia. The subduction zones between them first produced ocean troughs with their associated arcs of andesitic volcanic islands. Then, when the continents collided, the islands and all the oceanic sediments round about were thrust up into the high plateaus and mountain chains of today. Remains of the underwater volcanoes and the island arcs now lie high up in the Karakorams in Kohistan, northern Pakistan.

FAULTS

If fold mountains are found at the destructive plate margins, or where destructive plate margins were once active, then constructive plate margins tend to produce a different kind of mountain.

As the new material rises from within the mantle the crust bulges upward with the pressure. The crest of the bulge splits and tilts away from the center. The rocks are rent by faults and, at the very top of the bulge, blocks subside along the fault lines. These fault-bounded valleys are known as rift valleys and are found along the crests of the ocean ridges. The rift valleys that lie in continental areas are more obvious and they mark the lines along which a new constructive plate margin is developing. The Great Rift Valley of East Africa, with its elongated lakes, is such a feature, as is Lake Baikal in central Asia. At each side lie mountains, bounded by faults, formed as the broken crust moves up and down adjusting itself to the movements.

The Red Sea shows what happens to rift valleys a few million years after they are formed. Here, the Arabian peninsula has split away from the African mainland, opening an embryo ocean between. The blocks at each side are tilted upward and

HIGHEST AND LONGEST MOUNTAIN RANGES

● The Himalaya-Karakoram range contains the world's highest peaks, including Mount Everest – 29,029ft (8,848m).
● The Andes are the longest mountain chain in the world, running 5,530 miles (8,900km) along the length of South America.

backwards. As a result, the only tributaries of the Nile flow in from the east, reflecting the general tilt of this part of the African continent.

The Voges and the Black Forest are block mountains, associated with the stretching of Europe as the Atlantic opened.

VOLCANOES

Volcanoes are often acknowledged as a third type of mountain. In fact, they are not really significant as a mountain type. Andesitic volcanoes lie in active fold mountain belts, and basaltic volcanoes are often associated with fault block mountains.

WHAT SHAPES THE LAND?

IT IS ONE of the rules of nature that as soon as any area of land is raised up in mountain building the forces of erosion begin to work on it to try to wear it back down again. The most significant agent of erosion is the weather. Geomorphologists — scientists who study the shape of the landscape — acknowledge two types of weathering.

PHYSICAL WEATHERING

In physical weathering it is the actual force of the rain falling from the sky, the blasting of the wind or the expansion of ice that does the damage.

Falling rain can dislodge loose soil particles, washing away farmland that has lost its natural cover of vegetation. On a grassy hillslope where the surface soil is held together by the grass roots it is washed downhill slowly in step-like terracettes.

In very dry areas, the wind can pick up the soil particles and blow them around as sandstorms. This is a highly abrasive medium and deserts are full of rocks that are polished by the wind, or sand-blasted into fantastic shapes. The process produces even more sand.

Where an area experiences winter frost, the water in a rock crack will freeze. The expansion of the ice will widen the crack and weaken the rock. Repeated freezing and thawing will eventually shatter a mountainside and form long slopes of jagged rubble called scree.

In hot areas, the range in temperature between day and night causes the outer layers of the rocks to expand and contract. They then peel away in a process graphically described as "onion-skin weathering." This process is assisted by a chemical reaction between the minerals of the rock and the infrequent rains of such areas.

Below A hillslope usually collapses in the form of a slump. The hill cracks into arc-shaped slices that move downward on a curved surface, tilting back as they go, breaking up into a tongue at the bottom.

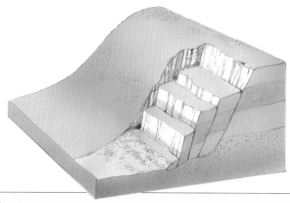

Below A landslip occurs when the beds of the rocks dip toward the slope. If the beds are lubricated by slippery beds of rock-like clay beneath, some of them may come loose and slip downward.

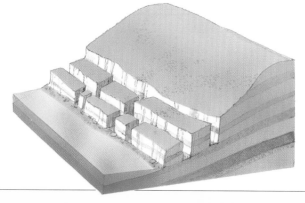

Left In Monument Valley, in the states of Arizona and Utah, the desert rocks have been polished by windborne sand to produce pinnacles, arches and many other strange and spectacular shapes.

Right Scree slopes, such as these in the English Lake District, form in cold damp climates. Angular chunks of rock are split from exposed cliff faces by the expansion of ice in pores and cracks.

RAPID TRANSPORTATION

● In 1925, a landslide occurred in Gros Ventre Canyon, Wyoming. Rocks dipping at a steep angle slipped along their bedding planes and 1,760 million cubic ft (50 million m³) of rock slipped down Sheep Mountain and blocked a river. This natural dam now holds back a lake 5 miles (8km) in length.
● In 1911, a landslip in the Pamir Mountains formed a dam 2,500ft (760m) high across the Murgab river. The resulting lake, now called Lake Sarezkoye is 45 miles (72km) long.

Below Soil creep occurs as loose soil inches its way down a hill. In the process, the underlying strata are pulled over.

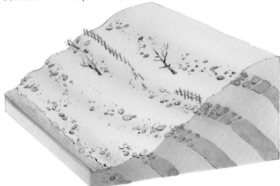

Below In a mudflow, a slope of loose material loses its coherence and slides downward. It may start as a typical slump structure but then disintegrates completely.

CHEMICAL WEATHERING

The chemicals of the minerals in rock often react with those dissolved in rainwater, breaking down the rocks in a process called chemical weathering.

Rainwater absorbs natural carbon dioxide in the air to form carbonic acid, and sulphur dioxide from industrial smoke to form sulphuric acid. The mineral calcite, which forms the bulk of the rock limestone, reacts with these to form soluble salts that are then washed away. Exposed limestone can dissolve into holes and caverns.

The mineral feldspar also reacts to the atmospheric acid. Granite is made up of feldspar as well as more robust quartz and mica. When the feldspar decays to clay, the other minerals fall loose. This usually happens along cracks and joints in the rock, and so in humid areas granite breaks up into blocks reminiscent of massive masonry, and local beaches have white quartz and mica sand.

TRANSPORTATION

These erosional forces tell only half of the story. Once the material of the land has been loosened the loose particles have to be moved away. This can be done by gravity, such as in soil creeping down a slope or in landslips. It can also be done by rivers, wind, glaciers, or sea currents (see pp.30-6). Eventually, the particles settle and become sediments — the raw materials for sedimentary rocks.

WHAT IS GROUNDWATER?

WE ARE ALL familiar with the rain as it falls from the sky. The spectacle of a river is common enough. Yet an important part of the Earth's water is invisible to us. It lies beneath the surface of the landscape, coating the soil particles and filling the pores in the rocks. This water is called the groundwater.

As the rain falls, some of it runs off across the surface, but much of it sinks into the ground, soaking the soil and accumulating at depth. At a certain depth, the soil and the rocks are so full of water that all cracks and pores are filled and they can hold no more. Hydrographers (scientists who study the movement of the Earth's water supply) call this region the zone of saturation. The top level of the zone of saturation is called the water table.

Below The amount of water of any area is controlled by the position of the water table or an aquifer. When the water table reaches the surface, a spring will flow. Wells have to penetrate the water table and reach saturated rock. A perched aquifer lies in a hill above a main aquifer.

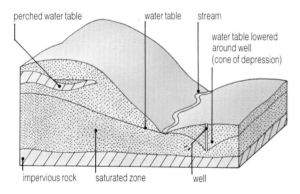

perched water table water table stream

water table lowered around well (cone of depression)

impervious rock   saturated zone   well

Above Calcite dissolved by groundwater in its passage through limestone can be redeposited in caves, as stalactites hanging downward or stalagmites growing upward.

SPRINGS AND WELLS

The water table and its position is a very important concept, both in physical geography and human geography. When the water table reaches the surface, as on a steep slope, the water seeps out of the ground and forms a spring. On the exposed sand of a beach at low tide there is a region of wetness that does not seem to dry out. This is the region that is beneath the water table.

In practical terms, the position of the water table must be known when digging a well. A well sunk to below the water table will have water in it. When the water is extracted more will flow in from the saturation zone around it. The water always takes time to seep from the surrounding rocks into the well and so the water table tends to be lower immediately surrounding a well that is being worked. Sometimes the water table in a well by the sea is lowered so much that the seawater flows in.

Sometimes a bed of rock that is saturated with water — a bed that hydrographers call an aquifer — is sandwiched between two impermeable beds. This may give rise to oases and wells in desert areas. If such an aquifer is exposed in mountain areas where rain is plentiful, and then runs underground beneath nearby lowlands it will produce a water supply and hence an oasis in any place where it appears at the surface. If a well is driven into it the pressure of water further up the mountains may cause the water to squirt out at the surface as an artesian well.

CAVE FACTS

● The cavern of Lobang Nasip Bagus in Sarawak is 2,300ft (700m) long, averages some 980ft (300m) wide and is nowhere less than 230ft (70m) high. The aircraft carrier USS *Enterprise* could fit into it, and still be able to fly its airplanes.
● The longest stalactite is in the Cueva de Nerja near Malaga, Spain – 185ft (59m).
● The longest stalagmite is in the Aven Armand, in Lozere, France – 95ft (29m).
● The longest column (combined stalactite and stalagmite) is in the Carlsbad Caverns, New Mexico, USA – 106ft (32.3m).

Below A limestone terrain can be riddled with caves and hollows, and also sinkholes which are made by surface streams disappearing underground. Sinkholes often collapse, forming elongated gorges and round depressions called dolines.

Bottom Water flowing over impervious rock may suddenly disappear underground when it meets a limestone. This is because it has dissolved itself a passage down through the soluble rock. At the water table it flows horizontally, eroding horizontal caves.

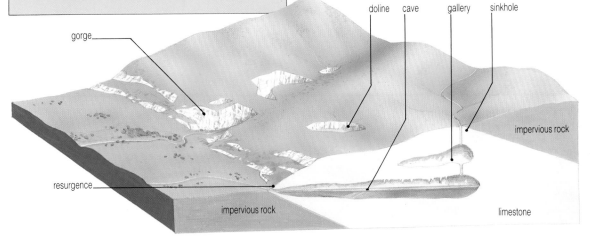

gorge · resurgence · impervious rock · doline · cave · gallery · sinkhole · impervious rock · limestone

LIMESTONE CAVERNS

The water flowing underground will have an effect on the erosion at depth, especially in limestone terrain. The carbonic acid in the groundwater decomposes the calcite that makes up limestone rocks. This happens most easily along cracks in the rocks, such as joints and bedding planes — the surfaces between individual beds. The result is the opening of cracks, usually at right angles to one another, and the breakup of the limestone mass into a series of rectangular blocks. Along the water table, the water may flow as an underground river, eroding a zigzag horizontal tunnel following the right-angled lines of weakness. If the water table drops for any reason, this tunnel is left as a dry gallery, and a new tunnel is eroded at the new level. The dissolved calcite in the water seeping through the rocks may be redeposited on the ceilings, walls and floors of these caves to form stalactites and stalagmites.

DO RIVERS FOLLOW A PATTERN?

AS WE HAVE seen, much of the rainwater that falls on the ground flows off over the surface. More of it sinks into the ground and reappears as springs. These waters unite and run downhill into any random depressions, forming streams that eventually grow into rivers and flow toward the sea. Geographers recognize three different stages of river formation.

YOUTHFUL RIVERS

The first stage of a river is seen in a mountain stream. It is full of splash and vigor as its waters hurtle down the slopes and over cliffs, forming rapids and waterfalls, on their way to the lower land. There is a great deal of energy expended here and this is used to scour away the streambed, eroding downward and carrying along boulders and stones. Deep V-shaped gorges are found at this stage and the river runs a zigzag course between high spurs that interlock like meshed fingers.

MATURE RIVERS

Then, in the lowlands, the river settles down to a more sedate pace. By this time it is much larger, as many youthful streams have joined it as tributaries. Much of the rubble and stones that have been carried along have now been ground down to sand and this is beginning to be deposited on the riverbed. Erosion is still taking place but it is largely balanced by the deposition.

The river here forms a broad flat-bottomed valley. It winds across the floor of the valley, changing its course from time to time. When it is near the valley sides it erodes the slopes back, forming high bluffs. The valley floor is formed of sediments that have been deposited by the river. As the river's course winds through these sediments the current is always faster on the outside of the curves eroding the bank away. On the inside of the curve, the sand and gravel that is being carried along is deposited as a beach. In this way, the curve of the river extends itself — a process called meandering. The fertile soils of a mature river valley are ideal for farming.

OLD MAN RIVER

When the river is almost at sea level, its current slows down drastically. It becomes too weak to do any more eroding and it can only deposit the material that it has brought this far. So, a flood plain develops. The river meanders across this, many of

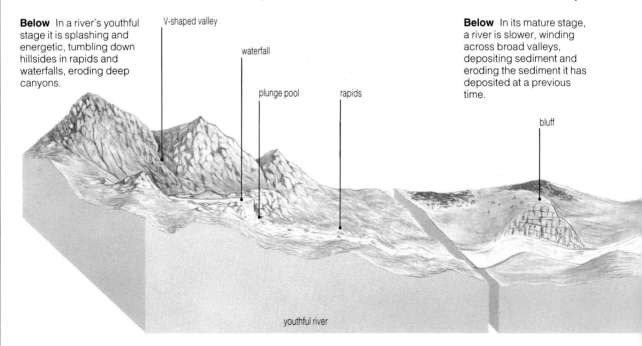

Below In a river's youthful stage it is splashing and energetic, tumbling down hillsides in rapids and waterfalls, eroding deep canyons.

V-shaped valley

waterfall

plunge pool

rapids

Below In its mature stage, a river is slower, winding across broad valleys, depositing sediment and eroding the sediment it has deposited at a previous time.

bluff

youthful river

the meanders being cut off as oxbow lakes. The whole area is liable to flooding and sediment builds up along the banks. As a river overflows its banks at times of flood, much of the suspended sand and mud is deposited close by as the current slows. The banks are built up above the level of the flood plain, as levees. The sediment on the riverbed may also build up with the result that the whole river runs at a higher level than the flood plain.

At the sea, if there is no sea current, the remaining sediment is deposited in the shallow waters. Levees can become elongated islands, splitting the river into individual branching channels. The result is a delta.

Flood plains are very attractive to settlers because of the richness of soil. However, flooding is always a problem although if it is annual, it can be welcomed as enriching the farmland, and built into the annual lifestyle of the farmers.

RIVER DISASTER

The world's worst recorded flood occurred in 1877 when the Hwang-ho in China burst its banks. Some 900,000 people perished.

Above In mountainous areas such as Switzerland there are many rivers in their youthful stage. Here, a deep gorge cut by a river's vigorous current can be seen on the skyline, and the frantic energy of the river shows itself in the white water of the waterfall and rapids.

Below In its old age, a river is sluggish and weak. It drops the rest of the material that it has brought down from surrounding hills and produces a broad flood plain.

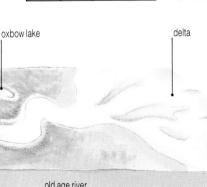

The networks of rivers and their tributaries can form recognizable patterns. Dendritic drainage **1** occurs when tributaries flow randomly into one another, producing a tree-like branching pattern. In a landscape of parallel ridges a trellis drainage pattern **2** may form. In this the rivers cut directly through the ridges or follow the valleys between, meeting one another at right angles. Radial drainage **3** forms where the rivers all flow away from one another as down the slopes of a domed structure.

flood plain

levee

meander

oxbow lake

delta

mature river

old age river

HOW DO COASTAL FEATURES FORM?

THE MAP OF our planet is constantly changing. Not only are the continents moving to and fro across its face, but the edges of the continents are continually being altered by the action of the sea.

EROSION

A wave thundering against a cliff or a sea wall can exert a pressure of some 100 tons per square foot (10 tonnes per m^2). The pressure can be three times as great during storms. This pressure compresses the air in the tiny pores of exposed rock, and when this air expands it does so explosively, breaking up the cliff face by hydraulic action. A corrosive action takes place as rocks and stones are hurled at the exposed cliff. The rocks and stones are also worn down by this action in a process called attrition. There are other, minor, influences such as chemical action of seawater on rocks; biological action through burrowing organisms, and frost action on the wet rocks in winter, which all have an effect.

Most of the erosive action takes place along joints and bedding planes, where the rocks are weakest, and most happens close to the tideline, where the force of the waves is greatest. A wave-cut notch develops, which undercuts the cliff until it collapses.

Where a coastline forms a series of headlands, the waves curve around and attack the headland from each side. The joints and bedding planes enlarge into sea caves. Sea caves from both sides of a promontory may merge and form a natural arch. As erosion continues, the lintel of the arch collapses, leaving the offshore part upstanding as a seastack. The material broken away by all this erosive action gathers as beaches between the headlands.

Left Coastal erosion is dramatically seen where vertical cliffs of chalk are worn away. The headland here on England's south coast is eroding back into a series of sea stacks.

Below Waves curve around to attack a headland from each side. Caves on each side meet up to form a natural arch, which eventually collapses to form a sea stack.

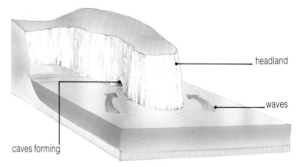

headland

waves

caves forming

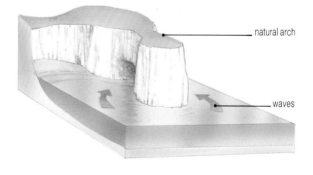

natural arch

waves

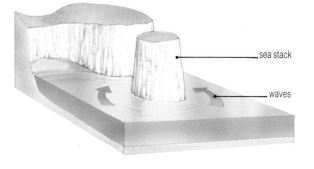

sea stack

waves

DEPOSITION

The sand, shingle, and other debris resulting from sea erosion is deposited nearby or carried away by currents and waves. Waves usually approach a beach at an angle, washing debris up onto it at an angle. When each wave withdraws it runs straight back down the beach, taking with it some of the debris. The next wave washes it up again at an angle. The result of this is a zigzag path, the net movement taking the sand and shingle along parallel to the line of the beach. Such a process is known as beach drift or longshore drift.

As the drift takes the sandy material along the coast it may reach an inlet. The sand builds out across the mouth of the inlet as a bay bar, cutting off a shallow lagoon. This may eventually fill up to form a marsh. Where such a bar builds out across a river mouth the constant current keeps it open. The resulting half-bar is called a spit. Currents may take the sand well past a headland and deposit it as a series of offshore bars, or barrier islands.

This beach drift is undesirable to coastal communities who need their beaches for the tourist trade, or to prevent waves from damaging buildings. Fences, called groynes, are erected across the beach, at right angles to the shoreline, to try to prevent it. Sand builds up on one side of the groyne but is swept away from the other.

Above There is a strong drift of sediment along England's east coast. To prevent the sand and shingle from being washed away, these groynes have been built out into the sea. The sediment builds up on the up-current side of each groyne, and is scoured away from the down-current side.

Left When sediment is washed along a coastline and meets a bay, it can be deposited across the bay as a bar or a spit. As the waves curl around the end of the spit the sediments are washed around and deposited there. The result is a spit with a hook-shape on the end.

DOES ICE INFLUENCE LANDSCAPE?

SNOW FALLS IN the highlands. In sheltered valleys where it has no chance to melt, the layers of snow build up year after year, compressing the lower layers and compacting them into ice. Under great pressure, ice is not the hard and brittle substance with which we are familiar. It deforms and flows like putty.

DOWN THE HILL

A compact mass of snow and ice in a highland valley begins to creep downhill under its own weight. It follows the line of any valley, becoming a river of slowly moving ice, called a glacier.

The great weight of a glacier grinds away at the valley bottom and sides, eroding it into a distinctive U-shape. The rocky material worn away is called moraine and is embedded in the ice, dragged along underneath or carried on top. The surface of a glacier, unaffected by the great pressures beneath, is normal brittle ice. As a glacier flows around beds or over humps, the surface cracks, forming deep crevasses. Ice pinnacles left by intersecting crevasses are called seracs.

Glaciers are continually fed by snowfalls in the mountains. Further down they begin to melt, the meltwater running down crevasses and hollowing

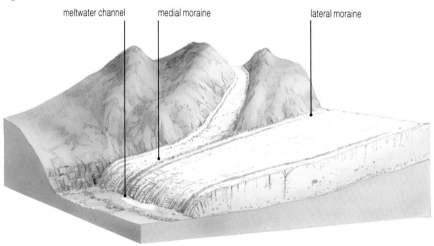

meltwater channel   medial moraine   lateral moraine

Right A glacier is a mass of ice that flows slowly downhill. In the mountains it may be white and fresh, but as it melts, the moraine shows through and lies on the surface giving the ice a dirty appearance further down. Lateral moraine becomes medial moraine as tributary glaciers merge. The glacier may be moving continuously downward, but when the rate of melting is high, the snout actually retreats uphill leaving a U-shaped valley.

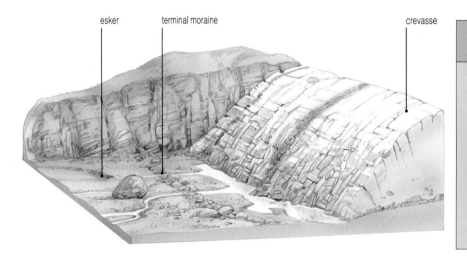

esker   terminal moraine   crevasse

GLACIAL LANDMARKS

● Drumlins are low, egg-shaped hills left by receding glaciers and molded by a subsequent one. Bunker Hill in Boston is the most famous drumlin in the United States.
● Long Island is a terminal moraine, left behind by a glacier during the last Ice Age.

Above The Gorner Glacier in Switzerland is a typical mountain glacier. It is much smaller than it once was. It has been slowly retreating up its valley since the end of the Ice Age 20,000 years ago.

Right During the Ice Age, the ice cap of the northern hemisphere came and went several times. At its greatest extent it reached down to the US and covered much of northern Europe and northern Asia.

ONCE IT MELTS

During the last two million years or so, the world suffered an Ice Age. The northern ice sheet spread south across much of North America, northern Europe and Asia, and valley glaciers crept down from the mountains in other parts of the world. This Ice Age has been over for 20,000 years, but we are still recovering. Areas such as Scandinavia are rising, bouncing up having been relieved of the weight of the ice.

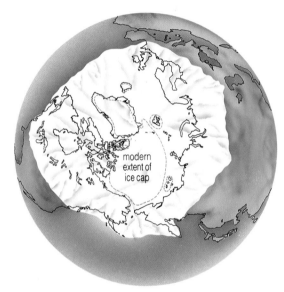

modern extent of ice cap

out ice caves beneath, until it emerges as a river at the snout. This meltwater is full of moraine and has a cloudy, muddy appearance. Deposits of shingle fill the valley downstream. The meltwater river cuts its way through banks of loose stone, splitting into separate channels and reuniting. This forms a pattern known as a braided stream.

ACROSS THE CONTINENT

The continent of Antarctica, and the huge landmass of Greenland, are both covered by enormous glaciers. Such continental glaciers are called ice caps or ice sheets, and spread outward toward the coasts rather than downhill. An ice sheet sitting on a continent adds greatly to the weight of the landmass, and presses the local crust down into the mantle.

In the areas once covered by ice, the remains of the ice sheets provide the major features of the landscape. Exposed rocks have been polished flat by the weight of ice, and show deep grooves — striations — gouged out by embedded moraine. The moraine itself lies thickly as deep deposits of clay, sand and boulders jumbled together, called boulder clay. This may form rounded hummocks called drumlins. The course of a river through an ice tunnel beneath the ice sheet may be marked by a sinuous ridge of moraine called an esker. The previous position of a glacier's snout may be marked by a line of rubble called terminal moraine, or by a kind of delta called a kame.

In the mountains, the deep U-shaped valleys show where the glaciers have been, and the tributary valleys at each side are left hanging at the top of the steep slopes.

WHAT IS THE ATMOSPHERE?

THE ATMOSPHERE CAN be regarded as being the outermost layer of the Earth's structure, the layer made of the lightest materials of all, the gases. Compared with the bulk of the Earth, the atmosphere is a very thin envelope around the outside. As with the solid part of the Earth, the atmosphere is divided into several distinct layers.

LAYER OF LIFE

As far as we are concerned the most important layer of the atmosphere is the lowest. From ground level up to about 36,000ft (11km) is the layer known as the troposphere. It represents only about 1.5 per cent of the atmosphere's volume, but it is so compressed by the layers of air above that it comprises about 80 per cent of the mass. In this layer, all air-breathing creatures exist. Here all the important meteorological events occur, and all the processes that result in the phenomena that we know of as weather.

THE LIGHTER LAYERS

Above the troposphere lies the stratosphere, the region traversed by high altitude aircraft. In this region lies the ozone layer, a layer in which the molecules of atmospheric oxygen combine with themselves to produce molecules of three atoms rather than the more usual molecules of two. It is the energy from the sun that brings about this reaction, and in doing so much of the harmful ultra-violet solar radiation is prevented from reaching the Earth's surface. There is increasing evidence that this ozone layer is vulnerable to man-made atmospheric pollutants. The stratosphere extends up to about 164,000ft (50km).

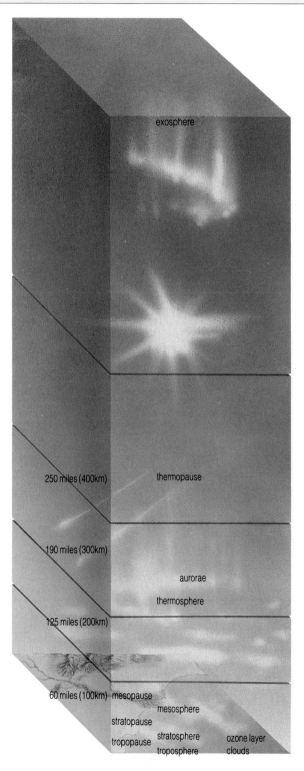

Left The atmosphere consists of various layers. At the bottom is the troposphere in which all life exists and all weather conditions are active. Above this, the gases become thinner and thinner, eventually fading off into space. These higher layers are defined by their ranges of temperature and other physical properties. In terms of mass, 80% of the atmosphere is in the troposhere; 19% in the stratosphere; and 1% in the mesosphere, thermosphere, and exosphere. In terms of volume, only 1.5% of the atmosphere is in the troposphere; 5.5% in the stratosphere; and 93% in the mesosphere, thermosphere, and exosphere.

Image labels: exosphere; 250 miles (400km); thermopause; 190 miles (300km); aurorae; thermosphere; 125 miles (200km); 60 miles (100km) mesopause; mesosphere; stratopause; tropopause; stratosphere; ozone layer; troposphere; clouds

Then up to about 262,000ft (80km) lies the mesosphere. The density of the air here is very slight, but it is still enough to stop space dust from penetrating. Particles of matter hitting the atmosphere from space are traveling so quickly that the friction produced as they pass through the upper layers of atmosphere burns them away. We see them as glowing streaks and call them meteors.

Above this is the thermosphere and then the exosphere, regions in which the air becomes thinner and thinner with height, eventually fading off into the vacuum of space at heights of over 430 miles (700km).

THE BOUNDARIES

Each layer is separated from the next by a boundary. Between the troposphere and the stratosphere is a boundary called the tropopause. Temperatures through the troposphere decrease with height until they reach the tropopause, and then they begin to rise again. They reach a maximum of about 10°C (50°F) at the stratopause — the boundary between the stratosphere and mesosphere — then fall off further up through the mesosphere. At the mesopause — separating the mesosphere and the thermosphere — the temperatures reach a minimum of about −120°C (−248°F) and begin to rise once more, and continue to rise through the thermosphere.

The incoming solar radiation is reflected and absorbed at different rates by the various layers until only about 50 per cent of it reaches the ground.

OZONE LAYER DEPLETION

Chlorofluorocarbon is a big word, but we are likely to use the substance every day. It is the inert gas used as a propellent in aerosol sprays, and as a refrigerant in freezers. Being inert it does not break down, so once it is released into the atmosphere it hangs around for centuries. If it drifts up to the stratosphere, it reacts with sunlight to form chlorine which interferes with the formation of ozone. Since 1989 it has become evident that this process is breaking down the ozone layer, especially in the still air over Antarctica. A loss of the ozone layer would be a serious matter in that it prevents ultraviolet radiation from reaching the Earth's surface; ultraviolet radiation that could cause skin cancers.

Below From the relatively low orbit – 100 miles (185km) – of the Space Shuttle, the Earth's atmosphere is seen as a misty haze along the horizon. The reflection from the water droplets makes the whole atmosphere look as if it is blue.

HUMAN INFLUENCE

There is a balance between incoming solar radiation and the amount of radiation reflected back to space. Some energy is absorbed by clouds, some reflected from them, some absorbed by the ground, some reflected from the ground's surface, some re-radiated from the ground and some of this re-radiation absorbed by the atmosphere. Human interference could upset the balance. After nuclear war, the atmosphere could be thick with dust. This would increase the amount of energy absorbed and reflected by the atmosphere. The result would be lower temperatures – a "nuclear winter."

With the build-up of industrial gases in the atmosphere, the energy re-radiated from the ground is absorbed into the atmosphere and causes temperatures to rise. This results in a "greenhouse effect."

IS THERE WATER IN THE ATMOSPHERE?

THE BOTTOM **36,000ft** (11km) of the atmosphere - the troposphere — sustains all the processes that produce the climates and the weather. Perhaps the most important concept in this, particularly as far as life is concerned, is the water cycle.

THE CIRCULATION OF WATER

The thing that makes the Earth unique in the Solar System is the fact that, at the surface, water can exist in its three phases — liquid, gas, and solid. Relatively small changes in conditions of temperature or pressure can change it from one to another: liquid water into gaseous vapor, or into solid ice. The process takes place continually. The vast liquid reservoirs are the oceans. Sunlight evaporates water from the ocean surfaces. Winds blow the vapor around, often over land. Pressures decrease as the vapor rises over mountains, or temperatures fall as the vapor passes over cooler areas. The vapor condenses into droplets, which form clouds, and the droplets coalesce into drops, which fall as rain. On the ground, the water flows over the surface or through the rocks, encountering the water table and emerging as springs. Streams gather the water and transport it downhill, eventually bringing it back to the oceans once more. This whole process is called the water cycle.

Yet this is a vast oversimplification. There are so many side branches to the cycle. There is evaporation from wet soil, from rivers and streams, and from lakes. Falling moisture may freeze and become locked up as glaciers for thousands of years. Plants take up groundwater in their roots and pass it back to the atmosphere through their leaves once they have used it. Rain may fall directly into the ocean.

THE RAINBOW

When white sunlight is reflected from a drop of water it is split into all the colors of the spectrum. Each color is reflected at a slightly different angle. When we see a raindrop in the distance on a sunny day we will see it as a particular color, depending on the angle between the sun, the raindrop and ourselves. A raindrop slightly further away will appear as a different color, because the angle will be different. A mass of raindrops in a shower will show up as a band of all the colors if the raindrops occupy the position in the sky where the angle is right for the colors to be reflected toward us: a rainbow appears.

THE PROPORTIONS

The proportion of the Earth's water that lies in the oceans is just over 97.2 per cent — in fact, most of it. A further 2.15 per cent lies frozen as glaciers and ice sheets; rivers and lakes contain 0.0171 per cent; ground water accounts for 0.625 per cent, while the atmospheric water vapor has only 0.001 per cent. All told it has been estimated that our planet holds 525 million cubic miles (1,360 million km^3) of water.

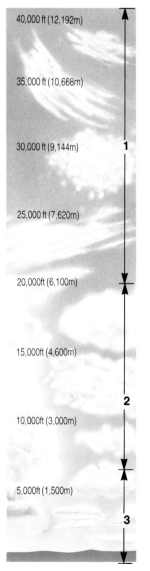

40,000 ft (12,192m)

35,000 ft (10,668m)

30,000 ft (9,144m) — **1**

25,000 ft (7,620m)

20,000ft (6,100m)

15,000ft (4,600m)

— **2**

10,000ft (3,000m)

5,000ft (1,500m)

— **3**

Left Clouds are classified by height and by whether they are layered (stratus) or heaped (cumulus).
1 High clouds, over 20,000ft (6,100m):
Cirrus Mares' tails, wispy and fibrous, made of ice.
Cirrostratus Cirrus merged into a continuous cover, forming a milky white sheet and a halo around the sun and moon.
Cirrocumulus Rounded masses in lines, or with a ripple effect.
2 Medium clouds, between 6,500 and 20,000ft (2,000 and 6,100m):
Altostratus A uniform layer, made of water droplets so it does not form a halo.
Altocumulus Broken into globules in a regular pattern as a "mackerel sky."
3 Low clouds, lower than 6,500ft (2,000m):
Stratus A low uniform layer that envelops hills, often drizzle.
Stratocumulus Like stratus, but thicker, containing dark bands.
Nimbostratus Thicker still, usually producing rain or snow.
Cumulus Fluffy clouds with flat bases and rounded tops.
Cumulonimbus Thunderclouds with low bases but bursting upward into the high cloud region and spreading out in an anvil-shape. Thunderstorms, rain, and hail.

CLOUDS

The droplets of water that condense to form clouds are so light that they can remain suspended in the atmosphere. Steady air can cause them to spread out to form flat clouds called stratus. Turbulent air can fluff them up into heaped clouds called cumulus. Very high clouds, forming at the top of the troposphere may be made of ice particles, formed directly from the water vapor without passing through a liquid phase. Clouds close to the ground are called mist and fog.

RAIN, HAIL, AND SNOW

In the turbulence of a cloud, the droplets can move up and down on convection currents. They coalesce and become drops large enough to fall as rain. Under very cold conditions ice crystals form. These are based on a hexagonal crystal pattern and may fall as snow. Sometimes, when the convection currents are very strong, the crystals melt and are refrozen to lumps of ice without a crystal form. The ice builds up layer by layer until it forms lumps too heavy to be supported. The resulting pellets of ice fall as hail.

Above In mountainous areas, the moisture in rising air may condense, because of the reduction in pressure, to form orographic clouds, as here around the Matterhorn.

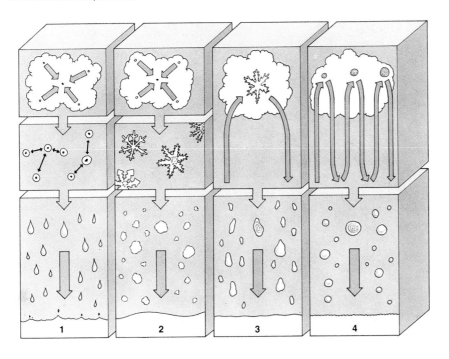

Left Precipitation is the name given to the fall of moisture from the atmosphere.
1 Commonly the atmospheric moisture will condense around dust particles to form droplets, and then drops that fall as rain.
2 Snow forms when ice crystals precipitate from very cold vapor. They aggregate in hexagonal shapes and form flakes.
3 Ice crystals may partially melt before reaching the ground, forming sleet.
4 Water drops flung up and down in turbulent clouds will freeze. Layers of ice will then build around them until they become so heavy that they fall as hail.

WHAT CAUSES THE WINDS?

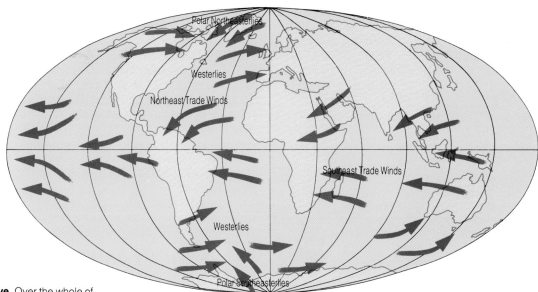

Above Over the whole of the globe, the winds form a general circulation pattern. The Trade Winds blow toward the equator, the Westerlies blow away from it and meet the polar winds.

Below The global circulation is driven by a series of convection currents. The Trade Winds blow toward the equator to replace hot air rising there. Cold polar winds blow from high pressure areas over the poles. Descending air at the tropics supplies both the Trades and the Westerlies.

polar high pressure

tropical high pressure

equatorial low pressure

tropical high pressure

polar high pressure

A HOT AIR balloon rises, carrying its passengers aloft, because the heated gases within the envelope have expanded and are less dense than the surrounding air. The same thing happens when air is heated naturally by the sun or by reflected heat from warm land surfaces. The rising warm air leaves a region of reduced atmospheric pressure beneath, and cooler, denser air flows in to restore the pressure balance. This is the origin of the winds.

GLOBAL CIRCULATION

On a global scale it is the shape of the Earth that determines the general circulation of the atmosphere. The hottest areas of the globe tend to be on the equator, where the sun is overhead. Hot air here is constantly rising, and winds are continually blowing in from north and south. These prevailing winds are known as the Trade Winds.

In the upper troposphere, the warm air spreads northward and southward and begins to cool. At about the latitude of the tropics — 23.5 degrees north and 23.5 degrees south — the cooled air begins to sink. On reaching the ground it spreads, some back toward the equator where it supplies the Trade Winds, and some toward higher latitudes. Over the poles lie the coldest regions of all. There is a constant high pressure region over the North Pole and another over the South Pole. Cold air is continually spreading outward. The cold winds produced meet the warmer winds spreading from the tropics giving rise to regions of unsettled conditions in the mid-latitudes.

COMPLICATIONS

Of course, it is not really as simple as this. For one thing the winds do not flow directly northward nor directly southward. The turning of the Earth produces what is known as the Coriolis effect.

The physical geography also has a strong influence. Hot areas are found in the middle of continents, giving rise to their own convection systems. Mountain ranges stand in the way of prevailing winds. High, icy plateaus produce areas of cold air that flows outward down the valleys as chill valley winds. Winds tend to blow from the sea during the day when the land heats up, and from the land at night when it cools. Seasonal changes disrupt the neat global pattern. And, especially along the boundaries between warm and cold air masses, temporary local disturbances produce the day-to-day variations that we call the weather.

WHAT IS THE CORIOLIS EFFECT?

The Earth's surface and anything on it at the equator is already moving eastward at a speed of 1,040mph (1,665kph) because of the Earth's spin. Further north or south, say at the latitude of the tropics, things are moving eastward at only 940mph (1,500kph). This is because toward the poles the Earth's surface is closer to its axis, and it does not travel so far in one revolution. (At the pole you would not be traveling at all — you would be spinning on the spot.) As a result, anything, including the wind, flying north or south from the equator starts off with a strong eastward push, and its path is deflected in this direction. The upshot of all this is that winds blowing toward the equator are deflected to the west, while those blowing away from the equator are deflected toward the east. Consequently, the Trade Winds are the Northeast Trades and the Southeast Trades respectively, the mid-latitude winds are called the Westerlies, and the cold polar winds blow from the northeast in the Arctic and southeast from Antarctica.

JET STREAMS

There are a number of very strong high altitude winds that blow from west to east. These may be 100 miles (160km) wide and up to 5 miles (8km) deep, and blow at heights of 30-40,000ft (9-12km). They are called jet streams and are often sought out by eastward-bound aircraft in order to save fuel.

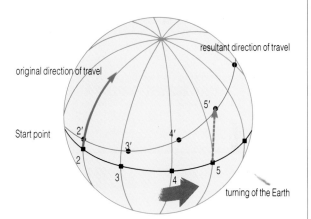

Below Prevailing winds – those that blow from one direction all the time – distort tree growth. Twigs and leaves grow in the direction of least resistance, so making trees lean over.

Above The Coriolis effect means that, after five hours traveling north, a wind from the equator will have been deflected to 5′ while its starting point will only have moved to 5.

WHY IS WEATHER CHANGEABLE?

IN THE NORTHERN hemisphere the cold north-easterlies (winds are always named after the direction from which they blow) sweep down from the icy Arctic ocean. The Westerlies blow from the warmer regions close to the tropic of Cancer. They meet in the mid-latitudes along a line called a "front."

FRONTAL SYSTEMS

Where they meet, the cold and the warm air masses slide by one another. Friction between the two masses causes them to curl and twist around, with a tongue of the warm air sweeping into the cold, and

Below At a warm front, a mass of warm air overrides a mass of cold. At a cold front, a mass of cold air creeps in under a mass of warm. As a warm front approaches, cirrus clouds appear at height, then come medium-high clouds like altocumulus, then low, rainy nimbostratus as the front passes. In the area of warm air there may be stable conditions. A cold front may lift air upward violently, producing thunderstorms.

Bottom 1 Cold and warm air masses slide by one another. **2** The friction between them distorts the boundary. **3** The warm air develops into a tongue that creeps into the cold air mass. **4** The entire system is moving continually eastward so that a place on the ground experiences a series of weather conditions. **5** Eventually, the cold front catches up with the warm, and the warm air is lifted clear of the ground to give an occluded front.

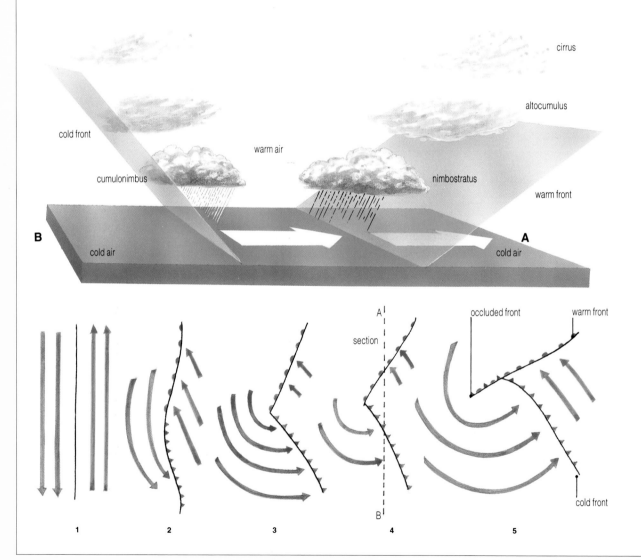

WIND SPEED

The traditional method of measuring wind speed is called the Beaufort Scale. Named after Admiral Francis Beaufort, hydrographer to the Royal Navy from 1829, it involves 12 points that define wind speed and wave height. It has now largely been superseded, and wind speed terms more often used are:

Term	Wind speed (knots)
Light	1–10
Moderate	11–16
Fresh	17–21
Strong	22–33
Gale	34–40
Severe gale	41–47
Storm	Over 47

Above The violence of a hurricane on the ground obscures any pattern to its actions. However, from orbit, the definite pattern of the air movements can be clearly seen. A very low pressure area in the center draws surrounding air in the form of very strong winds, thrown into a spiral by the Coriolis effect.

the cold air sliding in beneath the warm. The cold air, being denser, lifts the warmer mass, and the moisture that the warm air contains condenses, first as clouds and then as rain.

This gives rise to the "frontal system," a kind of huge eddy, which is the keystone of the daily weather in the mid-latitudes. The tongue of warm air intruding into the cold moves constantly eastward. The line along which it advances is called the warm front. It brings with it progressively lower clouds and then rain. The cold air catching up behind advances along the cold front, which may bring heavier rain. At the heart of the eddy is an area of low pressure and the winds constantly spiral into it — in a counterclockwise direction because of the Coriolis effect. Understanding frontal systems is important to people in North America, Europe, and Asia — all regions of convergent air masses.

HURRICANES

In tropical regions, the differences between high pressure areas and low pressure areas can be very great indeed. A warm area may produce a rapidly rising air mass over a tropical ocean. The rapid condensation of rain from this mass causes it to warm up even more, accelerating the process. Moist winds spiral inward and upward producing wind speeds of up to 190mph (300kph), towering clouds and torrential rain. The result is a hurricane. Hurricanes generally drift westward and when they reach land terrible damage results.

TORNADOES

A tornado is a similar phenomenon on a smaller scale. It begins with a violent updraft of air in a thundercloud. The updraft becomes so strong that it reaches down from the base of the cloud toward the ground. It forms an intense spot of very low pressure. The typical cone shape is visible because of the sudden condensation of moisture in the winds spiraling up it, and also because of dust and debris dragged upward from the ground. A tornado may last for several hours and travel for up to 300 miles (480km) before dissipating. Winds at the center may reach 400mph (640kph). As the low pressure center passes over a building, the relatively high air pressure in the building causes it to explode outward and the debris is scattered by the winds. Passing over the sea, a tornado will drag up water from the surface as a waterspout.

How do we Define Climate?

IF WEATHER IS the day-to-day change in atmospheric conditions at a particular place — by atmospheric conditions we mean humidity, rainfall, wind speed and direction, air pressure, temperature, and so on — then climate can be defined as the average of these conditions over a long period of time. The conditions that determine the global wind pattern also control the climates of the world.

WIND-DEFINED CLIMATES

As we have seen, the fact that the sun is directly overhead at the equator means that there is a permanent region of low pressure there, where hot air is constantly rising. The Trade Winds blowing into this low pressure region bring moisture with them from the oceans. This whole complex is called by climatologists the Intertropical Convergence Zone (ITCZ). The moisture falls as torrential daily rain as the air rises, resulting in the typical hot wet equatorial conditions with tropical rainforests.

The cooled equatorial air then spreads north and south, and where it descends, at about the latitudes of the tropics, all moisture has gone. Dry tropical zones of high pressure develop and as a result desert belts are found along the tropics.

Between these two extremes of wet and dry hot conditions the climate is a mixture of the two. As the relative position of the sun in the sky moves north and south with the seasons, so do these climatic belts. Between the equator and the tropics the conditions are hot and wet at one time of year, and hot and dry at another. Trees do not do well under these circumstances but grasses do.

In some places, particularly around the Indian ocean, the local geography disrupts this pattern. The great landmass of Asia heats up in the summer and winds from the ocean blow inland, bringing heavy rainfall to India and Southeast Asia. In the winter, the situation is reversed. The cooling continent produces a high-pressure area and cold dry winds blow outward to the ocean.

THE EFFECT OF GEOGRAPHY

In latitudes higher than the tropics the pattern is less well-defined. The climates become dependent on the distribution of land and sea as well as the global circulation.

World climates

- tropical rainy climate
  - equatorial rainforest
  - monsoon
  - tropical rain savanna
- dry climate
  - desert
  - steppe
- warm temperate climate
  - dry summer (Mediterranean)
  - dry winter
  - no dry season
- cool temperate climate
  - dry winter
  - no dry season
- polar climate
- highland climate

On the western coasts between latitudes of about 30 and 40 degrees north and south, the land is under the influence of the dry tropical high pressure conditions during the summer, but during the local winter the Westerlies move into the area bringing rainfall with them. This defines the so-called Mediterranean climate as found around the Mediterranean sea and in California in the northern hemisphere, and in southern Chile, South Africa, and southwestern Australia in the southern.

In the same latitudes on east coasts the winter Westerlies blow from the continental interior and so winters are cold and dry. New England and Japan have such a climate.

Between latitudes of about 40 and 60 degrees, the climate is very variable being under the influence of the frontal systems developed between the cold polar winds and the Westerlies.

Above Climate boundaries are indistinct and so climates are classified in many different ways. The classification often encompasses the natural vegetation as well, since the two concepts are closely related. Perhaps the most popular classification is the Koppen system which has been in use since 1900.

EXTREMES

The interiors of continents tend to be dry and show extremes of temperature. They are a long way from the moisture of the oceans and a long way from any modifying effect produced in more coastal regions by warm and cold ocean currents.

In the extreme north and extreme south, summers are short and winters are long and extremely cold. The prevailing cold winds blowing from the poles are dry and so there is little rainfall.

CAUSES OF CLIMATE CHANGE

Climates may change for a number of reasons. The tilt of the Earth's axis in relation to the sun may not be constant, and may fluctuate over thousands of years. The output of energy from the sun may vary from time to time. Or dust in the atmosphere, produced by volcanoes, may trap some of the sun's warmth. It is also possible that human interference could lead to global warming and long term climate change.

WHERE ARE THE RAIN FORESTS?

THE TROPICAL RAIN FORESTS, the hot steamy jungles of romantic literature, lie in the equatorial belt. Along the Intertropical Convergence Zone the high temperatures and constant rainfall produce ideal growing conditions. The Earth's equator is like a great greenhouse. Plants grow in profusion, scrambling over one another and reaching up towards the light.

The annual rainfall can be as much as 80in (2,000mm), and the surface run-off from the daily downpour produces huge rivers that drain vast areas of land. The Amazon in South America, the Zaire in central Africa, and the Mekong in Southeast Asia are the obvious examples.

THE NATURAL HOTHOUSE

The constant high temperatures — usually about 26 or 28°C (79 or 82.5°F) — vary by less than 3 degrees throughout the year. As a result there are no seasons and the vegetation grows all the time. Trees are evergreen, shedding their leaves and regrowing them at random.

Biologists recognize several layers of tropical forest. The tallest trees are known as the emergents.

These can tower up to heights of about 330ft (100m) and are supported in the soil by buttress roots. Below the crowns of the emergents the remainder of the trees spread their branches, intermeshing to form a continuous canopy. The leaves here are deployed to catch as much of the sunlight as possible. Epiphytes and creepers hitchhike to the light by clinging to the trunks and boughs of more sturdy plants. Down through the levels of greenery the sunlight is progressively absorbed so that below the canopy is a hot gloom. Little in the way of undergrowth grows in the darkness of the tropical

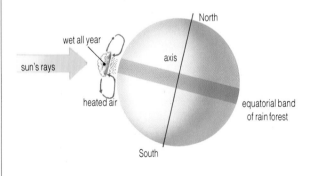

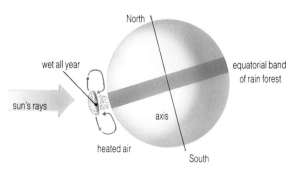

Left At all times of the year, the area close to the equator is almost directly beneath the sun's position in the sky. Here the constant rise of heated air brings moisture in from north and south and causes the rains.

Above The daily rain and unremitting heat of the equatorial regions acts like a gigantic greenhouse, producing prolific vegetation that grows as steamy forests.

A VALUABLE RESOURCE

Tropical rain forests cover only 8 per cent of the Earth's land surface but they make up about 50 per cent of all growing wood and are home to 40 per cent of the Earth's species of animals and plants Nearly 25 per cent of all medicines known to the West have been derived from tropical rain forest plants. By 1991, 50 per cent of the world's natural tropical rain forest had been cut down. If this continues, it will all be gone by 2020.

forest floor. Only when a great tree falls does light stream through a gap in the canopy down to the ground. Seeds immediately germinate and young shoots reach up to take the place of the fallen giant. The newly-formed gap does not last long, and soon a new tree has spread its leaves and branches, and the forest floor is again in a misty twilight. By riverbanks, where the sun can reach in from the side, the canopy reaches right down to the water's edge, forming what is called a gallery forest. Mahogany, ebony, rosewood, and greenheart are typical tropical forest trees, with mangroves growing in swamps and along riverbanks.

LIFE ABOUNDS

With such growing conditions the variety of plant life is enormous. Many different plants live in a very small area. Such a wide variety of plants means many different foodstuffs as well, and so evolution has produced numerous types of animals that can live there. Insects and other invertebrates abound. All kinds of birds, including hummingbirds, parrots, and toucans, many of them gaudily-colored, inhabit the branches. Amphibians, reptiles, and mammals are mostly climbing types, with long fingers and toes, and sometimes prehensile tails. Many have stereoscopic vision so that they can judge distances accurately as they leap from branch to branch. Monkeys, apes, sloths, iguanas, and frogs are typical tropical tree dwellers. Some, such as flying squirrels and gliding lizards, have developed the ability to glide from tree to tree. On the forest floor, the largest animals such as peccaries and capybaras are usually pig-sized. Anything larger would find difficulty in squeezing between the trunks of the densely packed trees.

A RAPIDLY DWINDLING HABITAT

Because of pressures of human population, the tropical rain forests are nowhere as extensive as they once were. Slash-and-burn agriculture, in which forest is cut down to make room for fields, and commercial logging, have meant that, by 1990, about half of the world's area of rain forest had been removed.

Tropical rain forests

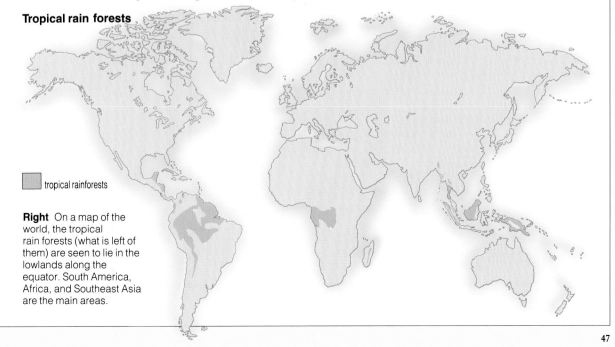

tropical rainforests

Right On a map of the world, the tropical rain forests (what is left of them) are seen to lie in the lowlands along the equator. South America, Africa, and Southeast Asia are the main areas.

WHERE ARE THE GRASSLANDS?

Temperate and tropical grasslands

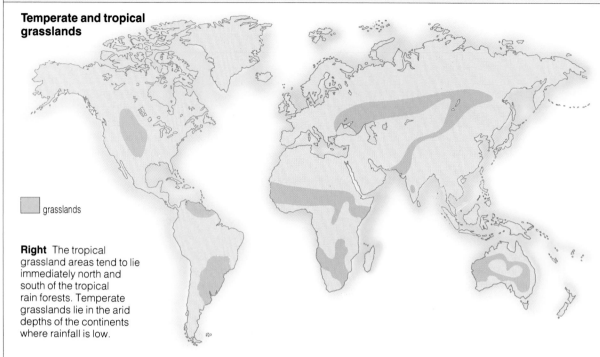

grasslands

Right The tropical grassland areas tend to lie immediately north and south of the tropical rain forests. Temperate grasslands lie in the arid depths of the continents where rainfall is low.

TO THE NORTH and south of the tropical forest belt is a region in which the heavy rains of the equator only fall at a particular time of the year. This happens during the region's summer, when the sun has moved overhead and has brought the Intertropical Convergence Zone with it. At other times of the year this region has a similar climate to the desert belts along the tropics of Cancer and Capricorn. In the long dry seasons, most trees would shrivel and wilt and the most successful plants are those that can hide underground awaiting the wet season and can then grow from underground stems and tubers. The grasses can do this, and the region between the equatorial rain forest and the tropical desert is the region of the tropical grasslands.

Grass can propagate itself from underground stems, and it sends up shoots from the safety of the soil. During the periodic fires that sweep such regions, the top of the plant can be burned away, but the growing point is safe underground and can send up new leaves directly afterward. Likewise, if the grass is eaten by animals it can grow again quickly. The only trees that do well in such conditions are acacias, baobabs, and drought-resistant palms. There is sometimes gallery forest (a stretch of forest along a river in an area of otherwise open country) along streams.

Below The tropical grasslands receive rain at only one time of the year, when the tilt of the Earth brings the Intertropical Convergence Zone (ITCZ) and its rain clouds into the area.

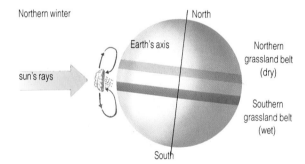

Northern winter

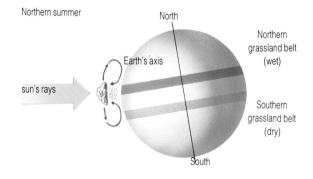

Northern summer

THE STORY OF OUR PLANET

The most famous tropical grasslands are those of Africa. They form the basis of the great nature reserves such as the Masai Mara in Kenya and the Serengeti in Tanzania. In South America, the southern tropical grassland belt is represented by the northern section of the Pampas. The Outback of Australia is partially desert and partially grassland.

Temperate grassland lies in the hearts of the northern continents. The low level of moisture here is due to the distance of the region from the sea, but the result is the same — grasses survive better than trees and bushes. The North American grasslands are the Prairies. In Asia they are called the Steppes.

GRASSLAND ANIMALS

Grassland supports its own form of animal life. Grass is a remarkably tough material to chew as it is full of silica. It must be like chewing sandpaper and consequently grass-eating animals (grazers) need very strong teeth and jaws to cope with it, and complex digestive systems to break it down. They also need long legs to allow them to run away from enemies for open grassland has few hiding places. A long face means that while the mouth is down chewing grass the eyes are still high up and can look for danger. Typical grassland animals, such as antelope, zebra, and kangaroos, all show these features.

PEOPLE AND GRASSLANDS

Like the tropical rain forests, the grasslands are dwindling because of human activity. Cereals, such as wheat, barley, and maize, form an important part of the human diet and the various types were developed from wild grasses. Most of the temperate grasslands have now been taken over to grow the crops needed for human consumption, and have become the great grain-producing regions of the Midwest of North America and the Ukraine of Eastern Europe.

Also, most of the domesticated animals used by humans are grass-eaters — cows, sheep, horses — and the grasslands are needed for their rearing. In parts of Africa, particularly the Sahel between the Sahara desert and the northern tropical grasslands, overgrazing by cattle is causing the widespread destruction of the habitat.

Below The zebra is a typical grassland-living animal. It has strong teeth and heavy jaws to pluck and chew the grass. The long face keeps its eyes above the level of grass while it is grazing. The long legs and hooves are built for running. The long neck enables its head to reach the ground while standing. The animal lives in herds, one reason being that while all are grazing some individuals are looking around for approaching danger. Such a danger could be hunting animals like the cheetah.

WHERE ARE THE DESERTS?

ADVANCING DESERTS

Desert occupies 33 per cent of the Earth's land surface. Environmental damage may soon raise this to 35 per cent. People have been creating deserts since settled agriculture began, but the process appears to be accelerating with the increase in population and consequent overuse of marginal lands. Desertification can be halted and land reclaimed if national resources and local communities are enlisted. In Kenya, for example, women farmers have been encouraged to plant trees to reduce wind erosion, create fuelwood and generate income.

Left Arid sweeps of bare stony ground are typical of desert terrain. The lack of moisture and plant roots means that the soil cannot hold together, and becomes gravel or sand.

Right Deserts lie where rainfall is slight. Tropical deserts are influenced by descending dry air. Continental deserts are far from the sea. Rain shadow deserts lie in the lee of mountains. Coastal deserts have their precipitation absorbed by cold currents.

WHERE THERE IS no water, no plants grow. The definition of a desert is as simple as that. Cold deserts are found in very high latitudes where the water that is present is permanently frozen and cannot be used by plants. However, the term is more often used for the hot, arid wastes found along the tropics.

Below The tropical desert belts lie along the tropics, in areas that are not affected by the wet conditions of the Intertropical Convergence Zone at any time of the year.

A VARIETY OF DESERTS

The main desert belts lie along the tropics, where dry air has descended having risen in the Inter-tropical Convergence Zone and dropped all its water there. In the northern desert belt lie the Mexican desert, the Sahara, the Arabian desert, and the arid portions of India. Along the southern belt lie the Kalahari of southern Africa and the Gibson and Simpson deserts of Australia.

There are other types of desert too. Continental deserts lie in the hearts of continents. Such areas are just so far from the sea that no rain can possibly reach them. The Gobi desert in central Asia is the most famous of these.

Or, when a prevailing wind blows off the ocean onto a mountainous coastline, the air rises up the mountains. In doing so its pressure drops and its moisture condenses and falls as rain on the leeward

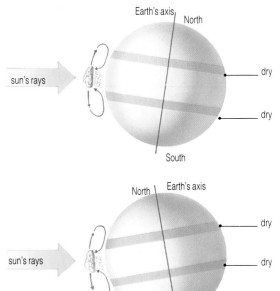

World deserts

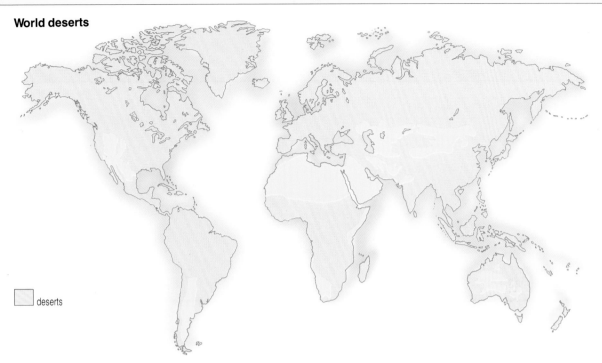

deserts

mountain slopes. Only dry air passes over the mountains to the continent beyond. The resulting desert is known as a rain shadow desert. Death Valley in California is an example.

Coastal deserts are found in hot regions where a cold ocean current runs close to the shore. This cold water cools the air above it so that any moisture it contains condenses to mist or falls as rain into the sea. Only dry air is left to blow over the land. The Namib desert on the west coast of southern Africa is one such desert. What plant life there is can subsist on the moisture of the sea mists. The Atacama desert in Chile, a narrow strip only a few miles wide between the ocean and the Andes, is another coastal desert. Further up the slopes there is plenty of vegetation, irrigated by the moisture of the clouds at that level.

DESERT LANDSCAPES

Rolling sand-seas of constantly shifting dunes with wind-borne wisps of dust streaming from the crests are the images usually generated by the term "desert." In fact, only about a fifth of the desert area of the world actually consists of sand like this. More common is the stony desert, where any fine material

has been blown away. Often, the finest material has been blown from between the larger stones and these have settled to form a crust — a so-called desert pavement — protecting the sand beneath from further erosion. The stones are polished on one side by the sand and dust blasting along in the wind. When they roll over, another side is polished resulting in a typical three-sided polished stone called a dreikanter. Exposed rocks are sandblasted into incredible shapes such as pinnacles and arches.

ANIMALS AND PLANTS

Any desert-living plant must be able to use what water it has efficiently and to store it. Thick stems and leaves act as reservoirs and these are usually defended by thorns or spines. Cacti fit this description well. Desert animals can usually obtain all their water from the food they eat — desert rats from the roots and tubers, and desert foxes from the flesh of the little plant-eaters. Most desert animals are nocturnal because of the severe conditions of the daytime.

Unlike other habitats, deserts are not under threat, although many of their plants and animals are.

WHAT IS THE TEMPERATE VEGETATION?

IN THE TEMPERATE regions of the globe, in latitudes higher than about 40 degrees, the seasons produced by the tilt of the Earth and its annual trip around the sun are most marked.

DECIDUOUS WOODLANDS

In the zone of deciduous forests, spring is the start of the year. Plants awake from their winter dormancy and leaves burst from their buds. Flowers open and the trees blossom, allowing insects and wind to pollinate and fertilize them for the new generation. Summer, when the sun is high in the sky and the days are long, is the main growing time. Leaves are at their most profuse, generating energy to allow the fertilized seeds to develop. In the fall, the days become shorter. The leaves, having done their work, are shed. The seeds and fruit have now developed to ripeness and these are dispersed. In the winter, it is cold, and no growth takes place. The plants are dormant. Seeds lie where they have fallen, waiting for the spring to come around again so that they can germinate and produce the next generation of plants.

Animals fit quite neatly into this scheme. The smallest do most of their eating in the summer and

Above The lush greenery of the deciduous woodland in spring and summer is in complete contrast to the red and yellow hues of fall and the stark bareness of winter.

Below Temperate woodlands lie mostly in the northern hemisphere. In the southern hemisphere, there is very little land in the latitudes where they would develop.

Temperate woodlands

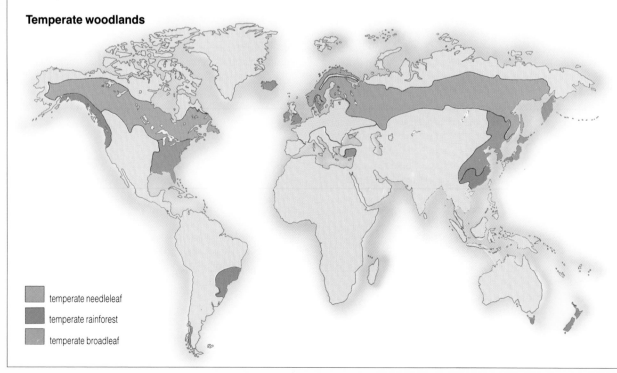

- temperate needleleaf
- temperate rainforest
- temperate broadleaf

the fall, when the leaves and fruits are growing and food is at its most plentiful. Often they store food against the leaner times to come. In winter they may hibernate.

The temperate regions have been settled since the dawn of history. As a result, their landscapes have been altered out of all recognition. Two thousand years ago northern Europe, for example, was covered with forest. Now it is all agricultural land or cities – the forests cleared away for pasture, croplands or settlements. Since these regions are major areas of industrialization the few woodland areas that are left suffer a great deal from pollution damage such as acid rain.

CONIFEROUS WOODLANDS

In the northern part of the temperate zone, the sun is low in the sky and winters are very harsh. Water is present, but exists only as ice for much of the year and cannot be used by animals and plants.

Only a few types of plant can tolerate these conditions, unlike the tropical rain forests in which just about anything can grow. This is the region of the coniferous woodland — vast areas of forest containing only one or two species of tree. Coniferous trees, such as spruce, pine, and fir, have tiny needles for leaves which minimize the loss of moisture through evaporation. They tend not to be shed in the autumn, saving the tree the energy of growing them again in the spring and ensuring that it is ready to catch the sunlight as soon as it appears. The conical shape of the trees allows snow to fall off easily.

Animals of the coniferous forests are cold-weather animals. As in the deciduous woodlands they do most of their eating when the food is available. Large animals, such as moose, build up layers of fat that will see them through the winter. Small animals, such as mice and squirrels, hide away seeds and nuts as winter stores.

CONIFERS AROUND THE WORLD

Most of the coniferous forests exist in the northern hemisphere. The Backwoods of Canada and the Taiga of Siberia constitute the largest areas of unbroken forest in the world. These do not exist in the southern hemisphere since most of the Earth's surface in the relevant latitudes is ocean.

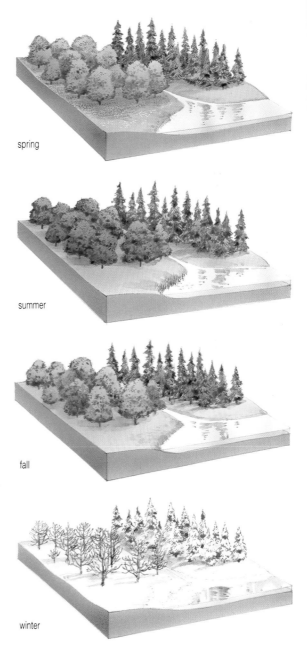

Below Deciduous woodland in the temperate latitudes changes with the seasons. The spring landscape of colored flowers and delicate new buds gives way to the summer green, and then to the fall hues of red, brown, and yellow, and finally the dark branches and trunks stark against the snow of winter.

spring

summer

fall

winter

WHAT LIVES IN THE COLD REGIONS?

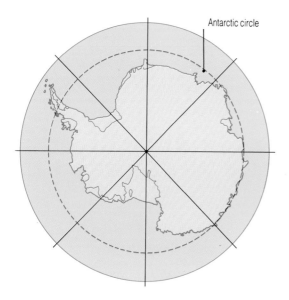

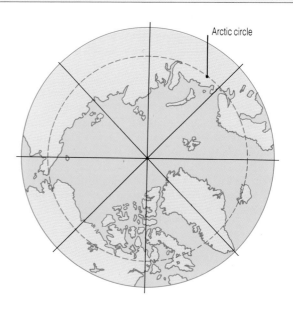

Above left The ice-covered continent of Antarctica lies at the South Pole. The surrounding ocean has little tundra land.

Above right The North Pole lies in the Arctic ocean, covered with floating ice. Surrounding lands have tundra areas.

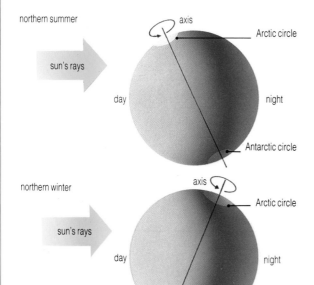

Above The tilt of the Earth means that there are regions in the far north and far south that receive no sunlight at all at some time during the year. Winter is cold and dark.

TOWARDS THE POLES, the sun becomes lower and lower in the sky. In the winter, the nights become longer. At a certain latitude, the Earth's surface is tilted so far from the sun that on at least one day of the year the sun does not rise at all. This latitude is at 66° 33′ and it defines the Arctic Circle in the northern hemisphere, and the Antarctic Circle in the southern. At the poles themselves there are six months of darkness followed by six months of daylight. During the summer at these high latitudes the days are very long and the sun may not set at all. However, the sun is always low in the sky and its power is very weak.

TUNDRA

In the northernmost wastes of the northern hemisphere continents the coniferous forests give way to bleak icy plains. These are covered with snow and ice in the gloomy winter, but during the brief summer they thaw out. However, the soil at depth remains frozen, and the meltwater from the surface cannot drain away, a condition known as permafrost. The result is a treeless summer landscape of lakes and marshes. The annual freezing and thawing heaves the topsoil around producing polygonal patterns and soil-covered mounds of ice called pingoes. This kind of terrain is called Muskeg in Canada, and Tundra in Siberia.

TUNDRA IN DANGER

Even the tundra is vulnerable to human interference. The heat from houses built on land underlain by permafrost may melt the permafrost beneath and cause the ground to collapse. The Alaskan pipeline, bringing oil from the oilfields in the far north, is built on stilts for much of its length to prevent this from happening. The low temperatures close to the poles mean that natural processes develop slowly. Any damage to wildlife in these regions would take a long time to recover.

Only hardy plants exist here. Mosses and lichens are typical, but hardy grasses grow, too. The only trees are scattered dwarf willows and mountain ash. If the conditions are hard for plants they are even worse for animals. However, during the brief summer, whole clouds of insects appear, breeding and growing in the temporary lakes, going through their entire life cycle as quickly as possible before the cold darkness returns. To take advantage of this insect bloom, birds flock up from less cold regions and feast, only to migrate back to warmer climates in the winter. The big mammals, too, are migrants. Reindeer and musk ox find enough to eat in the mosses and lichens during the summer but winter in the coniferous forests further south. This pattern is the basis of the way of life of the Lapps who follow the reindeer herds throughout the year.

POLAR CONDITIONS

In the extreme north and extreme south, near the poles, temperatures can fall as low as $-88°C$ ($-126°F$) and nothing lives. The Arctic Ocean in the north is permanently covered by a sheet of ice 160ft (50m) thick. Around the edges, the sea is fertile enough to support shoals of fish which are hunted by seals which are, in turn, hunted by polar bears. The Arctic Ocean is almost landlocked, and the only access to the other oceans of the world is through the Bering Strait and between Norway and Greenland. The constant influx of river water from the continents keeps the ocean fairly fresh.

In the southern hemisphere, the continent of Antarctica is covered by ice. The barrenness of the land contrasts dramatically with the abundance of sea life. Upwellings of cold water around the continent and the continuous summer sunlight produce a bloom of algae. This supports a huge population of shrimp-like krill. Fish feed on the krill and are in turn eaten by seals and penguins.

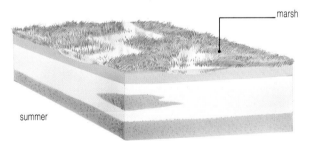

marsh

summer

permafrost

winter

Left The permafrost layer comprises soil below the surface that remains frozen, even if the surface soil thaws out. This means that the surface water cannot drain away in the summer.

Above Summer in the tundra is characterized by wet marshy areas. Spiky grasses, lichens, and mosses are about the only plant types. In winter, this would all be covered by snow.

WHAT LIVES WHERE?

IT IS OBVIOUS that different types of animals live in different habitats — swift climbing fruit-eaters live in the tropical rainforests, long-legged grass-eaters live in the grasslands, migrating moss-eaters live on the tundra, and so on — but there are other factors that influence the distribution of animals around the globe.

Throughout Earth's history the geography has determined the distribution of animal life. During Triassic times, when all the continents were joined together to form Pangaea, the same dinosaurs lived everywhere. Then, when the supercontinent split up, different creatures evolved on different parts. Two-footed duckbill dinosaurs lived in North America in Cretaceous times, while long-necked plant-eating sauropod dinosaurs thrived in the separate continent of South America. Different mammals then evolved on North and South America, and the South American types only became extinct as they were replaced by North American types when the two continents were joined a few million years ago.

MANY REALMS, MANY POPULATIONS

These principles are still active today. Different groups of animals live in different areas isolated from the others by barriers of one sort or another. The science here is called zoogeography and it was first studied by Victorian naturalists who established a number of zoogeographic realms.

The Ethiopian Realm encompasses most of Africa. Its boundaries are the oceans at each side of the continent, and the Sahara desert in the north. The strip of Africa along the Mediterranean sea actually belongs to the Palearctic Realm (the realm that covers Europe and northern Asia) because the animals there are more related to the animals of Europe and Asia than to those of the rest of Africa. The Oriental Realm with its tigers and elephants is essentially Southeast Asia, separated from the Palearctic Realm by the Himalayas. North America is the Nearctic Realm. It shares many types of animals, for example reindeer, with the Palearctic Realm because until recently the two were joined across the Bering Strait. The southern boundary of the Nearctic Realm is the Mexican desert. South of this in Central and South America is the Neotropical Realm with its llamas and anteaters. The most isolated of all is the Australasian Realm,

Zoogeographic realms

Nearctic realm

Neotropical

Above The world can be divided into six zoogeographic realms. In each, the indigenous animal life is different from the animal life of the others. The barriers between the realms consist of oceans, mountains, and deserts — all inhospitable to the land-living animals on which the zoogeography concept is based.

covering Australia, New Zealand, and parts of the East Indies. This realm has evolved by itself for so long that it contains animals like the marsupial kangaroos and koalas that exist nowhere else.

EVOLUTION'S LABORATORIES

Islands are a special case. Many, like Madagascar or the Galapagos, are little zoogeographical realms of their own. The animals have had time to evolve in total isolation from the rest of the world and are found nowhere else. This makes them very vulnerable to introduced species and to human activities.

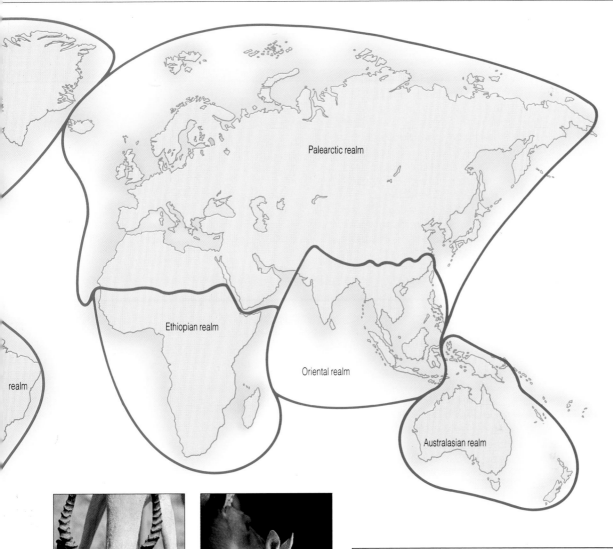

Above The antelope is an Ethiopian realm grazing animal with a long face, strong teeth, powerful jaws, high eyes, and heat-shedding ears.

Above The Australasian grazer is the kangaroo. Its long face, strong teeth, powerful jaws, high eyes, and heat-shedding ears are due to convergent evolution.

THE HUMAN COMPLICATION

In the last few thousand years the human influence on the distribution of animal and plant life has been profound. Exploration and colonization have broken down the traditional zoogeographic barriers, usually to the detriment of the native wildlife. For example, Palearctic rabbits were taken to the Australasian Realm, Palearctic horses were introduced into the Nearctic Realm where they had become extinct millions of years ago, and Nearctic gray squirrels were introduced into the Palearctic Realm where they have been rapidly replacing the native red squirrels.

WHAT IS SOIL?

THE VEGETATION OF our world would not exist if it were not for the covering of loose material that we call the soil. It acts first as a foundation, holding the plant in position by the roots, and second, as a reservoir for the water, storing the essential minerals needed to keep the plant alive. Finally, it acts as a blanket, helping to keep the ground at a fairly even temperature.

When the forces of erosion and weathering act on naked rocks the rocks begin to crumble. This is the starting point of soil. Once vegetation begins to grow in it, dead plant material is added. Water passing through leaches out salts from the top layers and redeposits them further down, or brings them up from the bedrock. Burrowing animals mix all this together. The result is a mature soil. It takes about 10,000 years for a mature soil to form.

SOIL PROFILE

The cross section of a typical soil shows a number of distinct layers. At the top is the humus layer. This consists of partially decayed plant material. Below this is the topsoil, in which humus is mixed in with the mineral material of the soil. Then comes the subsoil, in which any minerals dissolved from the topsoil are redeposited because of lack of oxygen. Below this lies a region of broken parent rock, which becomes increasingly solid the further down it goes until we reach the parent rock itself. This whole vertical section is called the soil profile.

Different conditions give rise to different soil types which are determined by climatic conditions rather than the underlying rocks. So, in warm humid regions, moisture can penetrate deep into the bedrock and react with the minerals there. Such regions tend to have much thicker soils than dry cold regions in which the rocks react only slowly to water.

CLASSIFICATION

Podzol is one of the main types of soil. This corresponds closely to the idealized soil profile, with the humus layer, the partially-leached topsoil, the mineral-enriched subsoil, and the broken bedrock. Podzols are found in cool, moist conditions. Brown forest soils are typical of temperate woodland regions and are rich in plant material, making them very valuable for agriculture.

World soils

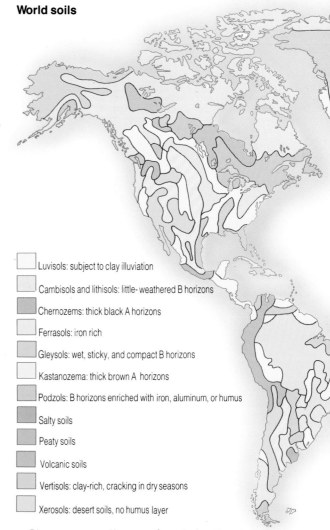

Luvisols: subject to clay illuviation

Cambisols and lithisols: little-weathered B horizons

Chernozems: thick black A horizons

Ferrasols: iron rich

Gleysols: wet, sticky, and compact B horizons

Kastanozema: thick brown A horizons

Podzols: B horizons enriched with iron, aluminum, or humus

Salty soils

Peaty soils

Volcanic soils

Vertisols: clay-rich, cracking in dry seasons

Xerosols: desert soils, no humus layer

Chernozem soils are found in the temperate grassland belts, where there is not enough rain to wash away the humus derived from the grasses. These very black, rich soils are good for growing wheat. Lateritic soils form in wet tropical regions where organic material and most of the minerals are rapidly leached away, leaving only red deposits of iron and aluminum oxides. These can bake hard in the sun and are useless for agriculture.

This is only a selection of the main types of soil. The study of pedology is a complex one. The pioneering work was done in Russia, which is why most soil types have Russian names. The United Nations Food and Agriculture Organization recognizes 106 different types in its classification adopted in 1974.

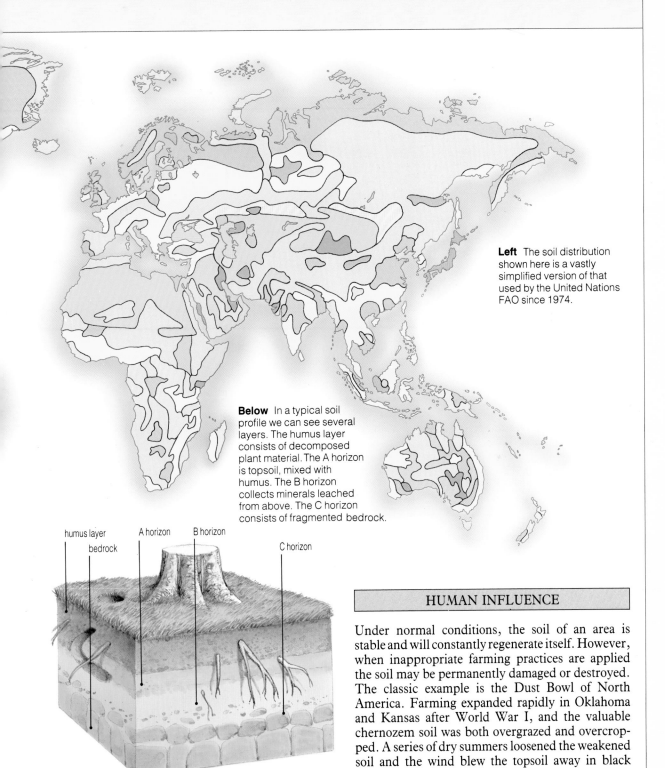

Left The soil distribution shown here is a vastly simplified version of that used by the United Nations FAO since 1974.

Below In a typical soil profile we can see several layers. The humus layer consists of decomposed plant material. The A horizon is topsoil, mixed with humus. The B horizon collects minerals leached from above. The C horizon consists of fragmented bedrock.

humus layer
bedrock
A horizon
B horizon
C horizon

HUMAN INFLUENCE

Under normal conditions, the soil of an area is stable and will constantly regenerate itself. However, when inappropriate farming practices are applied the soil may be permanently damaged or destroyed. The classic example is the Dust Bowl of North America. Farming expanded rapidly in Oklahoma and Kansas after World War I, and the valuable chernozem soil was both overgrazed and overcropped. A series of dry summers loosened the weakened soil and the wind blew the topsoil away in black blizzards.

WHAT LIES BENEATH THE OCEANS?

ALMOST THREE-FOURTHS of the Earth's surface is covered by water. Most of this forms the three major oceans: the Pacific with 65 million square miles (170 million km^2); the Atlantic with 36 million square miles (95 million km^2); and the Indian with 28 million square miles (74 million km^2); and the smaller Arctic ocean with 5 million square miles (12 million km^2).

The topography of the ocean floor can be divided into a number of distinct features, all formed as a result of plate tectonics.

A BIG MYSTERY

It has often been said, with some justification, that we know more about the surface of the moon than we do about the ocean floor.

Below The continental slope sweeps down from the continental shelf to the continental rise and the abyssal plain. Although the gradient of the continental slope is regarded as steep, this is only a relative term. The actual gradient is shown on the diagram at the bottom.

Right The ocean ridge is constantly being built up and out. The volcanic action emplaces new plate material that then moves away. The continual volcanic action in the form of hot mineral-rich springs called smokers has been observed by deep-sea survey vessels.

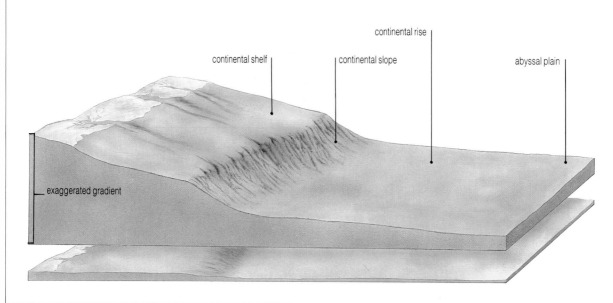

continental rise

continental shelf   continental slope   abyssal plain

exaggerated gradient

THE MAJOR FEATURES

The shallowest features are the continental shelves which are basically the edges of the continents that happen to be awash. Continental shelves are typically only about 330ft (100m) deep. They can be very broad, as off the northwest coast of Europe, or so narrow as to be almost nonexistent, as off the western coast of South America.

The edge of the continental shelf is marked as the continental slope, where there is a sudden steepening of the seabed. This is a steep drop, with a gradient of typically 370ft per mile (70m per km) to the ocean depths. At the bottom, the slope becomes much gentler because of the accumulation of debris that has slid down the continental slope. This is the continental rise.

The floor of the ocean is called the abyssal plain. This is between 11,500 and 18,200ft (3,500 and 5,500m) deep and lies in permanent cold darkness. There is very little land-derived sediment down here. Most of the floor-covering is derived from the shells of microscopic floating organisms. This sediment is called ooze and principally consists of calcite or silica. Fine clay from windblown dust and debris dropped by drifting icebergs also finds its way into the deep ocean sediments.

The sediments thin as they reach the oceanic ridges. These are the tectonically active areas where molten rock is welling up from the mantle and new plate material is being emplaced. The ridges rise from the depths of the abyssal plain to about 13,200 to 3,300ft (4,000 to 1,000m) below the surface. However, occasionally the oceanic ridge will rise above the surface of the ocean, to form islands such as Iceland and the Azores.

The oldest parts of the abyssal plains are those closest to the ocean trenches which show where the ocean plate is being pulled down into the Earth's mantle and being destroyed. The deepest point is the Marianas Trench in the western Pacific, some 36,200ft (11,033m) below sea level.

CORAL REEFS

A coral reef is a distinctive formation found in warm, shallow seawater. Around an island, where the water is clear and warm, corals may grow in the shallow water. When they die they leave behind their limy shells, and the next generation of corals will grow on the skeletons of those that went before. Such a structure builds to the surface of the sea and surrounds the entire island, forming a fringing reef.

As time goes on, the island may subside. The coral continues to grow from its original foundation, but the island will become smaller. The result is a small island surrounded by a broken ring of coral reef: a barrier reef. Finally, the island may sink from view entirely, but the reef will continue to grow as an isolated ring — an atoll.

Below The classic coral reef sequence – the fringing reef attached to an island, the barrier reef just offshore of an island, and the atoll with no obvious island in sight – are seen throughout the Pacific.

Volcanoes form and move away from the sites of eruption by plate tectonics. Although an old volcano may slowly be eroded and eventually disappear completely, coral reefs continue to grow.

fringing reef   barrier reef   atoll

WHAT IS SEAWATER?

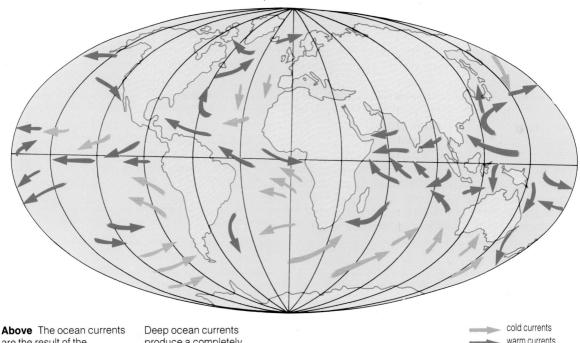

Above The ocean currents are the result of the prevailing winds blowing across ocean surfaces.

Deep ocean currents produce a completely different pattern.

→ cold currents
→ warm currents

SINCE THE FIRST moisture condensed on a parched young Earth, soluble minerals have been dissolved from the rocks. Over time, these dissolved minerals have built up in the oceans and now result in the saltiness (salinity) of the sea.

SALTINESS

The saltiest regions of the ocean tend to be warm, landlocked seas where evaporation is high, such as the Mediterranean and Red Seas. Here the concentration of salts may be above 38 parts per thousand. The coldest seas in the world, in the Arctic and Antarctic, are the least salty, with a concentration of below 33 parts per thousand. In the Arctic ocean this is accentuated by the constant influx of the great northern rivers.

Although the salinity varies from place to place, the composition of the salt is very stable. Chlorine and sodium are the principal components, at 19.5 and 10.8 parts per thousand respectively, and these elements together form common salt. All the other components together make up less than 3 parts per thousand.

WAVES

Seawater is in constant movement. Wind blowing over the surface causes the water particles at the surface to move in a vertical circular motion producing an undulation at the surface that we call the waves. When a wave reaches shallow water, this vertical circular motion is distorted and the wave curls over and breaks into surf. Although the waves travel for vast distances over the oceans, it is just the disturbance that is traveling, and not the water itself.

CURRENTS

The prevailing wind pattern has a yet more widespread influence on the movement of the oceans as it produces the global circulation of ocean water that we call the ocean currents. Near the equator, the Northeast and Southeast Trade Winds bring water together from the northeast and southeast. When they meet they move together westward, producing westward-flowing equatorial currents in the Pacific, Atlantic, and Indian oceans. On meeting the continents, these currents spread north and south, becoming the warm currents often encountered off east coasts. These include the Gulf Stream of the northern Atlantic, the Brazil Current of the southern Atlantic, and the Kuroshio off Japan. The water returns toward the equator down the eastern sides of the oceans, forming cold currents, such as the Humboldt current off Chile, the Californian current off North America, and the Benguela current off the southwestern coast of Africa. On the large scale, this movement causes a circular motion of the seawater, called a gyre. Each gyre typically occupies half an ocean. Around Antarctica the Westerlies produce a continuous cold current called the West Wind Drift. All this oceanic movement is complemented at depth by a system of deep ocean currents that is just as complex.

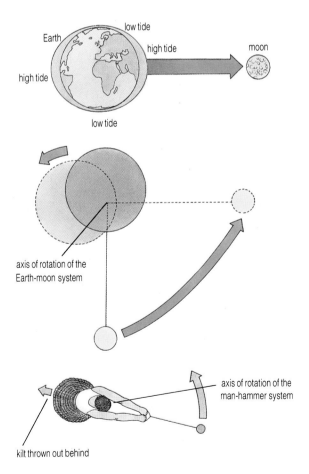

Left The high tide on the side of the Earth facing away from the moon is caused by a similar set of forces to those that throw out a highlander's kilt as he throws the hammer.

Above Disturbances of the water at the sea's surface can be carried thousands of miles by the prevailing wind. On reaching shallow water, these build up to form the breaking waves.

TIDES

The moon does not simply go around the Earth. The Earth and the moon actually go around one another, the axis of rotation being somewhere within the Earth not far from the Earth's center. The result is that the Earth is continually swinging around, and the water on its surface is thrown out as a bulge on the side away from the moon. The effect is rather like that seen at the Highland Games in Scotland when a man is throwing the hammer. His kilt is thrown out behind him as he swings the hammer around. The Earth's movement therefore produces high tides on the side of the Earth away from the moon. Another high tide is produced on the side facing the moon because of the moon's gravitational attraction. As the Earth turns within these water bulges, any place will experience two high tides in a day. The sun has a similar, but less strong, influence and this reinforces the moon's influence twice a month when all three bodies are in line, and works against it when they form a right angle. This accounts for the high high tides (spring tides) and low high tides (neap tides) twice a month.

PACIFIC AND ARCTIC OCEANS

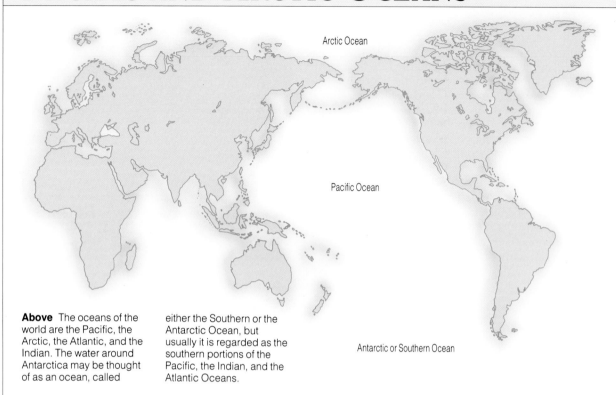

Arctic Ocean

Pacific Ocean

Antarctic or Southern Ocean

Above The oceans of the world are the Pacific, the Arctic, the Atlantic, and the Indian. The water around Antarctica may be thought of as an ocean, called either the Southern or the Antarctic Ocean, but usually it is regarded as the southern portions of the Pacific, the Indian, and the Atlantic Oceans.

AN ASTRONAUT VIEWING the Earth from orbit over the equator and at a longitude of about 180 degrees, would see no land. The Earth would appear to be a planet consisting totally of water. This is because he or she would be over the center of the Pacific ocean, an area of water that covers 35 per cent of the planet's surface and constitutes about half of the world's ocean area. It has an average depth of 14,050ft (4,280m) and a volume of 173,625,000 cubic miles (723,700,000km^3).

A SHRINKING OCEAN

The Pacific ocean is gradually becoming smaller. The ocean ridge system, forming the East Pacific Rise that runs from California southward to the Southern ocean and then turns west disappearing into the Indian ocean to the south of Australia, is continually generating new plate material. However, the whole Pacific basin is ringed by destructive plate margins and the surrounding continents are gradually encroaching on the ocean area. These plate margins are seen as the ocean trough system that runs from New Zealand, along the north of the East

A FAST TURNOVER

● The East Pacific Rise is the world's fastest spreading constructive plate margin. The plates at each side are separating at about 6in (15cms) per year.
● The speed of encroachment of the continents at the destructive plate margins on each side is greater than this, and so the Pacific is shrinking.

Indies, splitting into several branches as it reaches up toward Japan, then to the Kamchatka peninsula and around the arc of the Aleutian islands. Beneath the coast of North America it becomes confused because the continent has overridden it, resulting in the earthquake-prone regions of California. Then it picks up again along the coast of Mexico and continues down the edge of South America. The earthquake and volcanic activity along this line has given it the name the Ring of Fire.

The oldest section of the Pacific floor is the part furthest away from the ocean ridge, the part that is disappearing down the Marianas Trench, and is about 135 million years old.

THE COLD ARCTIC

If the Pacific Ocean is the warmest and largest of the oceans, the Arctic Ocean is the coldest and smallest. It has an average depth of 3,250ft (990m). Much of it is covered by floating ice, and since for most of the year this is continuous with the surrounding continents, navigation is very difficult. An oceanic ridge begins near the island of Severnaya Zemlya and slips out between Spitzbergen and Greenland to become continuous with the Mid-Atlantic ridge further south. A warm current, the remains of the warm North Atlantic Drift, flows into the Scandinavian side, setting up a gyre. This becomes a cold current that sweeps southward past Greenland carrying away icebergs spawned from the Greenland icecap.

Left The islands of the tropical Pacific – the South Sea islands of romantic literature – are often surrounded by coral reefs. An aerial photograph of the islands of the Tonga group shows very clearly their fringing reefs which are attached to the shorelines of the islands.

Below From whatever angle we look at the Earth we tend to see much more ocean than land. The Pacific Ocean covers more than a third of the Earth's surface, although it used to be even larger. The Arctic Ocean is the smallest of the oceans. It is also the coldest and the least salty.

PACIFIC ISLANDS

Scattered across the Pacific ocean are strings of islands. Most of these are the remains of hot-spot volcanoes. Hawaii is the best example, with its currently-active center on its largest island, and progressively older islands stretching away to the northwest. Below sea level, the line is continued as the Emperor Seamount Chain. To the southeast of Hawaii new volcanic activity has been detected on the seabed, showing where the next center will eventually develop.

Further south, the Society island chain, although not currently active, shows the same features. It also demonstrates nicely the development of coral reefs, with no reef on the youngest island Meheita in the southeast, a fringing reef around Tahiti and Moorea, barrier reefs around Raiatea and Bora-Bora, and a string of older atolls stretching away to the northwest.

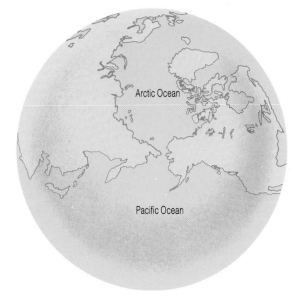

Arctic Ocean

Pacific Ocean

ATLANTIC AND INDIAN OCEANS

BESIDE THE COMPLEXITIES of the Pacific Ocean, the structure of the Atlantic is simplicity itself. It is a growing ocean with a constructive plate margin up the center and no destructive margins to speak of. The shape is symmetrical, with the constructive margin forming the Mid-Atlantic ridge, and the opposing coastlines forming a neat jigsaw fit, particularly in the south. Small destructive margins lie where individual continents are jostling one another, as in the Caribbean, the Mediterranean, and the South Sandwich islands to the east of the Falklands. Islands along the center line show where the ocean ridge peeps from the surface, as in Iceland, the Azores, and Tristan da Cunha. The ridge turns to the east in the very south, rounds the tip of southern Africa, and becomes continuous with the ridge system of the Indian Ocean.

Water circulation is quite simple, with an equatorial current producing a classic gyre in the southern half. The northern gyre picks up water warmed in the Gulf of Mexico and carries it northeastward to western Europe, and even on to the Arctic as the North Atlantic Drift.

The average depth of the Atlantic is 10,930ft (3,330m) and its volume is 77,235,000 cubic miles (321,930,000 km³).

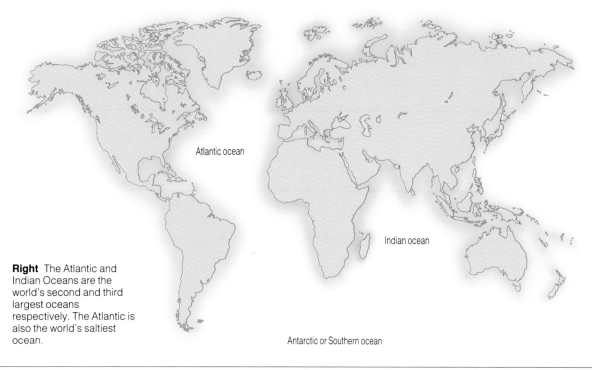

Atlantic ocean

Indian ocean

Right The Atlantic and Indian Oceans are the world's second and third largest oceans respectively. The Atlantic is also the world's saltiest ocean.

Antarctic or Southern ocean

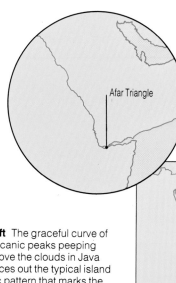

Afar Triangle

Below and left The Red Sea is an ocean in embryo. A constructive plate margin – part of the Indian Ocean system – has split the continent apart, seen by the jigsaw fit of the opposing coasts. The only overlap is in the southern corner where the Afar Triangle of Ethiopia is actually made of oceanic crust.

Left The graceful curve of volcanic peaks peeping above the clouds in Java traces out the typical island arc pattern that marks the line of a destructive plate margin. Along this line, the plate of the northeast Indian Ocean is being drawn down beneath that of Southeast Asia and destroyed.

Arabian plate

African plate

Afar triangle

INDIAN OCEAN

The Indian Ocean, by contrast, is quite complex. Its average depth is 12,760ft (3,890m) and its volume is 70,086,000 cubic miles (292,131,000km³). Its structure is dominated by a plate margin system that lies across the basin like a canted T. The crosspiece of the T begins in the Red Sea where it is pushing continents apart and producing an infant ocean. It emerges from the Gulf of Aden and crosses the ocean, becoming continuous with the ridge of the Pacific to the south of Australia. The upright of the T comes in from the Atlantic around the coast of southern Africa and meets the crosspiece about halfway along.

The ocean basin is the result of Gondwanaland's tearing itself apart. About 70 million years ago, India broke free of Africa, moved northward and eventually collided with Asia. This action tore away other chunks of Africa and left them scattered across the ocean floor behind it. Today they are seen as the islands of Madagascar and the Seychelles, and as submerged portions of continent like the

Agulhas and the Mascarene Plateaus. The islands of the Indian Ocean are derived from continental material and are predominantly granite, contrasting with those of the Pacific which are nearly all volcanic.

To the northeast of the Indian Ocean is a destructive plate margin. The northward movement of the northeastern plate of the Indian Ocean basin has brought it up against the continental plate of southeast Asia and part of the destructive plate margin of the western Pacific. The Java Trench has formed along the plate margin and the East Indies has developed as the associated volcanic island arc.

Because of the monsoon climate of the continents to the north, the circulation pattern of the Indian Ocean is as complex as the geology. In the northern summer, the circulation is fairly normal, with a gyre forming in the north and one in the south. In the northern winter, when the wind blows out of the Asian landmass, the northern system breaks down into a series of irregular mini-gyres.

WHAT IS A MAP?

A MAP IS basically a picture of the Earth or a part of the Earth as seen from above. A map has many uses; it can be used for navigation or for showing distributions. The earliest civilizations made maps of one kind or another, but the science of cartography really started with the ancient Greeks in the second century AD.

The earliest maps were merely drawings of the ground as visualized by travelers and explorers. The development of printing and engraving in the fourteenth century improved the science of map-making, as did the great voyages of exploration. In the eighteenth century both Britain and France initiated large scale topographic surveys of their countries.

The modern mapmaker, or cartographer, has a whole range of technology at his or her disposal. Laser beams, infrared equipment and microwaves are used for accurate measurements on the ground. Aerial photography — or photogrammetry — can record the features of large areas. Satellites can observe and measure vast regions at once, encode the results and transmit them to Earth, where they are fed into computers. The computers can then draw the maps automatically.

MAP TYPES

The early maps were primarily designed as topographic maps, to give a picture of the distribution of physical features such as mountains, rivers, and towns in a particular area. To show as much detail as possible on a sheet, conventional symbols were adopted. Mountains were originally shown by an outline of a mountain range. Then hachuring was introduced, in which fine lines were drawn following the slopes. Hill shading is another technique, and this shows the distribution of light and shade that would be produced if light fell upon the land from a particular angle. The most practical and common way of showing relief is, however, by using contours. A contour is a line that joins all points of equal height. A mountain is shown by a concentric pattern of lines, showing different altitudes.

Maps that do not show the topographic features of the area are known as thematic maps. These are used to show such things as soil types, rainfall or land use. They can also be used for statistical purposes, to show for example per capita income or the age ranges of populations.

THE OLDEST MAP

The oldest artifact that can be interpreted as a map is an engraved clay tablet from Babylon, dating from 3000BC. It records the ownership of land.

Early maps were designed to give a detailed picture of physical features. Mountains, rivers, and towns were shown by symbols which resembled the actual features as closely as possible.

Gradually, outlines of mountain ranges were modified by hachuring, where fine lines indicated the mountain slopes.

Hill shading is an elaboration of hachuring, showing the distribution of light and shade. This gives the impression of light falling upon the actual land. Modern maps, however, generally employ contour lines.

MAP SCALES

Distance on a map is usually indicated by the scale. This may be shown as a scale bar against which distances on the map can be measured directly. A proportional figure may also be used, such as 1:100,000. This means that one unit on the map would represent 100,000 units on the ground. The larger the scale of the map the more details can be included on it. Town maps are usually of a scale of 1:1250 or 1:2500, while world maps will have much smaller scales such as 1:50,000,000 or 1:1000,000,000.

Right A sextant is an instrument used for finding one's position on the globe, and so is one of the mapmaker's tools. At midday exactly, the operator takes a sighting of the sun and the horizon through the built-in telescope. An adjustable mirror superimposes the two images. A calibrated scale then measures the position of the mirror and hence the angle between the sun and the horizon. This gives the angle of latitude of the operator.

Below By 1630, the date of this map of Africa, cartographers were producing quite accurate maps.

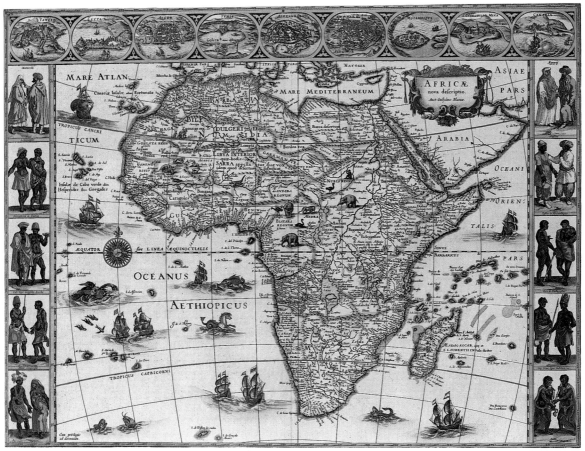

HOW IS THE WORLD MEASURED?

POSITION ON THE Earth's surface is usually determined by a reference to longitude and latitude.

Latitude is the distance measured in degrees north and south of the equator. Imagine a protractor placed at the center of the Earth, with the 0 degree line aligned with the equator and the 90 degree line pointing to the pole. The latitude of a point on the surface is the angle measured at the center of the Earth between that point and the equator. A particular value for the latitude defines a circle on the surface of the globe — a circle that will be smaller than the equator. Such circles are known as parallels.

Longitude is the distance measured in degrees east and west of a line that passes through the North and South Poles and the Greenwich Observatory near London, a line called the Greenwich Meridian or the Prime Meridian. In theory, a protractor is laid flat on the latitude of the equator with the 0 degree line pointing to the Greenwich Meridian. Distance around the equator can then be marked out in degrees east and west as far as 180 degrees at the other side of the world from the Greenwich Meridian. Lines joining these equatorial points to the poles are called the meridians. Any point on the globe's surface can then be located by stating its meridian and its parallel.

PROJECTIONS

The big problem of mapmaking is that a curved surface — the surface of the Earth — must be represented on a flat sheet of paper. In small-scale maps showing, say, a single town, this is hardly a problem, but it is a serious consideration when we want to portray continents. Something always has to be distorted, whether it be the distances, directions, or shapes. The device used to rectify the problem is called a projection.

The theory of projection is quite simple. Imagine the Earth as a transparent sphere, with the lines of longitude and latitude drawn on it. Now place a light at the center, and hold a sheet of paper against the outside of the sphere. The longitude and latitude lines will be thrown as shadows upon it. This is the basis for the map. In practical terms the work is done mathematically.

There are three main types of map projection. In the cylindrical projection, the theoretical sheet of

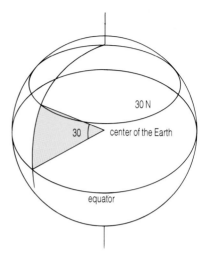

Above The lines of latitude are determined by angles between points on the surface of the Earth measured from the Earth's center.

Below Peters projection is based on equality of scale and area, thus eliminating any bias towards Europe.

equal area projection

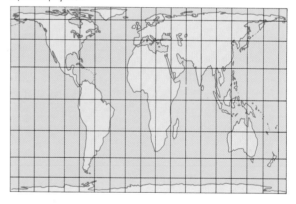

paper is rolled around the globe, touching it at the equator. Mercator's projection, named after the Flemish geographer and cartographer Gerhardus Mercator (1512–94), is the typical cylindrical projection. In a conical projection, the paper is rolled into a cone, touching the globe along a particular line of latitude. In an azimuthal, or zenithal, projection, the paper is flat and touches the globe at a single point. The theoretical light usually originates at the center of the globe — the gnomonic arrangement; but it may originate at a point on the globe's surface — giving the stereographic arrangement — or even at infinity — the orthographic arrangement.

CHOICE OF PROJECTION

Each projection has its own use. If the map is to be used for navigation it is important that directions are accurate. A cylindrical projection would be suitable, since this produces parallel meridians, north is always in the same direction, and angles can be measured accurately. Such a projection distorts areas badly, however, enlarging them toward the poles. A map in which areas are important, such as one showing density of population, must use a projection which does not distort area. Most atlases use a conical projection, although some consider equal area gives a more accurate view.

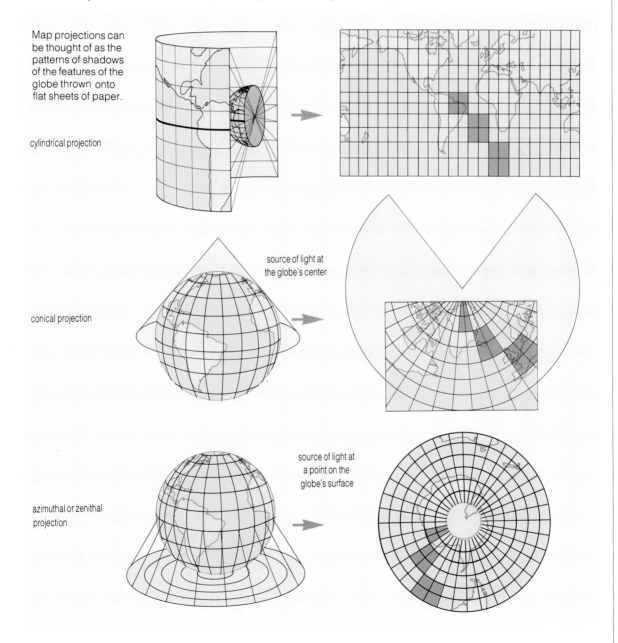

Map projections can be thought of as the patterns of shadows of the features of the globe thrown onto flat sheets of paper.

cylindrical projection

source of light at the globe's center

conical projection

source of light at a point on the globe's surface

azimuthal or zenithal projection

HOW IS THE WORLD SURVEYED?

BEFORE IT IS POSSIBLE to draw a map, the area to be mapped must be measured, or surveyed. There are three main elements in this — the measuring of distances, the measuring of angles, and the measuring of heights.

DISTANCES

The simplest way of measuring distances is by using a tape or a surveyor's chain. But this is only useful over small distances and has its drawbacks when measuring uneven ground. Mechanical devices such as tapes and chains may also expand or contract with changing temperatures and humidities.

Distances can also be measured optically by using a theodolite which is a kind of small telescope mounted at a particular point through which the surveyor spies a graduated rod mounted at another point. The graduation marks on the rod can be aligned with a scale in the theodolite and the distance between the two points calculated.

More modern distance-measuring devices use light or radio waves. A light is beamed at a reflector and the time taken for the beam to return to the source is recorded, that time being proportional to the distance between the instrument and the reflector. Radio waves can be used in the same way, but over larger distances and through low atmospheric visibility.

ANGLES

The theodolite is also used for measuring angles. The instrument can rotate around vertical and horizontal axes and the angle of rotation on either axis can be read off from a graduated scale. In this way the angular distance between two distant survey points can be measured.

HEIGHT

To measure height, the classic technique is one called leveling. This uses a device like a theodolite, but fixed horizontally. It is sighted on a graduated rod held vertically at the point where the height is to be determined. The height can be measured from the graduation on the rod. The height of another point may be measured by moving the instrument to that point and sighting on the same graduated rod.

COORDINATING THE READINGS

Triangulation is the technique used to combine all these measurements. From one point the angles of several other points are measured. Then they are measured from another point at a measured distance away, each reading serving as a check on the one

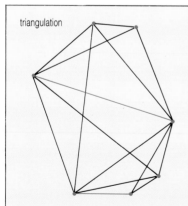
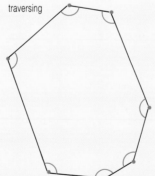
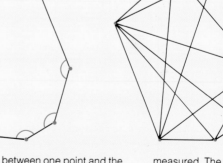

Surveying a piece of land involves the measurement of angles and distances. In triangulation, a base line is measured accurately and the angles of various points are measured from it. The surveyor then has enough information from which to calculate the distances between these points. In traversing, the distances between one point and the next are measured, as are the angles between them. In trilateration, there is no measurement of angles, but all the distances are measured. The angles can then be worked out mathematically from these.

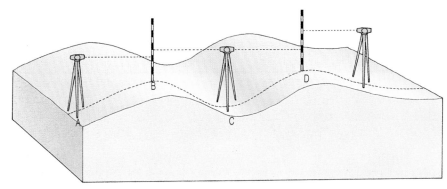

Above Heights can be measured by leveling. An instrument with a horizontal line of sight is set at a point of a known height – point A. It is then aligned with a graduated staff at another point – point B. The height reading on the staff is recorded. From point C the reading on the same staff is also recorded, as is the reading on a staff at point D. Sequential readings over a large area will give the differences in elevation of all the points.

before. Trilateration is a similar technique but distances are measured from which the angles can be calculated. A combination of triangulation and trilateration gives the techniques of traversing, using both angles and distances.

A similar technique is the plane table survey. A sheet of drawing paper is mounted on a horizontal table at a known position. An instrument called an alidade, which is a sighting telescope attached to a straight drawing edge, is placed on it and aligned with a graduated rod at another position. The direction is drawn along the marked edge, and the distances calculated from the calibration of the instrument.

MODERN TECHNIQUES

Nowadays most mapping is done by aerial photography. A series of photographs is taken from an aeroplane, each one overlapping the next. A pair of adjacent photographs will show the overlapping relief in three dimensions and skilled cartographers can interpret the results.

Satellite photography, and measurements using laser beams between the Earth's surface and an orbiting instrument, are bringing modern cartography into realms of accuracy never before visualized.

A SIMPLE SATELLITE

The simplest mapping and navigation satellites consist merely of a mass of heavy metal, such as uranium, covered with reflectors. Their great mass gives them a very stable orbit, so that their position in the sky is known accurately at any time. Laser beams reflected from them can give readings so accurate that even the rates of continental drift can be recorded.

HOW DID AGRICULTURE DEVELOP?

THE EARLIEST HUMAN societies were hunter-gatherers. The strongest members of the group travelled over large distances chasing food animals, while the others combed the territory for berries, roots, fruits, and other plant foods. A tribe that pursues such a way of life spends most of its time finding the food and has little time to develop a culture. Such a practice is still carried out today, among people who inhabit very harsh environments, such as the Eskimos or Inuit of northern Canada, Bushmen of the Kalahari desert and the Semang of the Malaysian tropical rainforests.

Eventually it was realized that the plants that were of the most use as food or as manufacturing materials were those which could be collected from where they grew wild, and planted in some convenient place close to the settlement. There they could be looked after and protected, and they could be harvested easily. Agriculture had begun. The development of this way of life defines the beginning of the Neolithic period of human culture — the New Stone Age.

The Neolithic cultures began in the Middle East some 12,000–10,000 years ago, where the first plants to be cultivated were wheat and barley. The fertile river plains of the Tigris, the Euphrates, and the Nile were exploited first. At about the same time, farming began independently in China where the main crop was millet. Tribes in north Africa farmed pearl millet and rice some 7,000 years ago and those in South America were growing maize and potatoes 3,000 years ago.

PRIMITIVE FARMING

The most primitive type of agriculture is called slash and burn. The natural vegetation of a small area is cut down and burned, and the plants needed for cultivation are grown in the cleared space. After the land is exhausted, the tribe moves on and starts again in another area. Today communities, such as the Boro of Amazonia, that still practice this type of farming, are causing serious damage to the few areas of tropical rain forest that remain.

The earliest cultivated plants were plants of tropical grasslands and for many thousands of years the rain forests were not exploited. Then, about 2,500 years ago, tropical forest food plants such as yams and bananas were brought to Africa from the forests of Malaysia and this led to agriculture being established within the rain forests.

Right The slash and burn type of agriculture, in which an area of virgin forest is chopped down and burned to make way for crops, is nowadays conducted on a much larger scale than at any time in the past. It is the major threat to the remaining natural rainforest, as here in Ecuador. However, any gain is temporary. The rain forest soil quickly loses its fertility.

Left Along the banks of the Nile the farmland was enriched by silt deposited by the annual floodwaters. For this reason, the Nile valley and floodplain, along with the other Middle Eastern river plains, were among the first areas to be cultivated. However, the climate is quite arid and during the dry season this fresh soil is often turned to dust and blown away.

SOIL PREPARATION

The digging stick and a light plough called the ard were invented sometime between 11,000 and 9,000 years ago and these helped to prepare the ground for the planting of food. Strong animals were domesticated and used for the heavy work.

In the wild, it is the environment, including the climatic conditions and the type of soil, that determines the kind of vegetation that will grow naturally at a particular place. Inevitably any farming will introduce an imbalance in this natural system, and so early farmers soon had to learn to control the environment of their planted crops.

A constant water supply is needed for the successful growing of crops which can be artificially supplied to cultivated land by irrigation. This is employed where the rainfall is too sparse for any crop growing, or where it is erratic and unreliable. It probably began when changing conditions decreased the water supply to a formerly well-supplied area. It is known that 5,000 years ago farmers along the Nile trapped its annual floodwater and channeled it to their fields.

A VALUABLE RESOURCE

● About a tenth of the land surface of the Earth is suitable for growing crops.
● About a fifth of the land surface is suitable for use as grazing land.

Intensive farming of one patch of land also meant that the nutrients of the soil were quickly used up. Chemicals like nitrogen, phosphates, and potassium are essential for plant growth. These could be replaced most easily by animal waste. In this way early farming developed alongside animal husbandry.

The result of the coming of agriculture was the establishment of a reliable source of food that was safe and easy to obtain compared with the chance and danger of the hunter-gatherer lifestyle. More time could be devoted to other activities, and culture and civilization could develop. It also produced an increase in the human population, and larger areas of the Earth came under cultivation.

WHAT IS MODERN AGRICULTURE LIKE?

WITH THE INCREASE in population that followed the development of civilization, farming had to become more efficient in order to supply enough food. Many types of agriculture are now found throughout the world. There are all kinds of factors that influence the type of farming that is carried on at a particular place. These include climatic factors, such as rainfall, evaporation, snow cover, temperature, length of daylight, and the risk of frost and damaging winds; geological factors, such as altitude and gradient, and depth and type of soil; and sociological factors, such as market demand, transport, government assistance, labor supply, and degree of mechanization.

TROPICAL AGRICULTURE

Many areas of the tropics are farmed on a small scale. The farms are based on small family units and worked without much mechanization. Subsistence crops, rather than cash crops, tend to be grown, and these may be rice in wet areas and millet in dry areas. Being subsistence crops they do not generate much profit and so there is no possibility of investing in much mechanization.

In wet areas, rice may be the most important food crop, and is intensively farmed. Swampland and

Above In the river plains of China, the waters have been channeled and used to irrigate rice paddy fields and fish ponds, making as much use as possible of the arable land and water available.

Above right The open plains of Europe and North America are intensely farmed for grain. The high degree of mechanization is evident in the use of a whole team of combine harvesters cutting a field of barley.

Left The forested mountain slopes of Bali in Indonesia are difficult to cultivate. Paddy fields are built as horizontal shelves into the slopes to hold the water that is essential for the growing of rice, grown as the food crop in the area.

river deltas are the ideal locations, but mountainsides may be terraced to hold back enough water for the planting. Only about 5 per cent of the rice grown is used as a cash crop.

Tropical cash crops are usually grown on plantations. These are often large estates originally established by colonial powers and worked with local labor but usually supported by American or European capital and management. Plantation crops include rubber, coffee, cocoa, tea, sugar cane, cotton, and tobacco.

TEMPERATE AGRICULTURE

There are more farming systems in temperate regions than in tropical areas. Peasant farming is still practiced in the Middle East, whereas intensive mixed farming, in which many types of crops are grown producing very high yields, is found in western Europe. Extensive monocultures devote large areas to a single crop, as in the wheat prairies of North America, and collective farming, in which all the land is owned and the labor is employed by the state, was the mainstay of the agricultural system of the USSR until the social and political upheavals of the early 1990s.

The main crops grown in temperate regions include the cereals wheat, barley, oats, rye, and maize, and "root" vegetables like potatoes.

NEW TECHNIQUES

The so-called agricultural revolution took place in Britain between 1750 and 1850 when the old inefficient practices were superseded. Four-year crop rotation was brought in, new crops such as turnips were introduced from abroad, and improved animal stock was developed. This all helped to feed the growing industrial population.

The green revolution of the 1960s involved the production of high-yielding crops and the use of machinery and artificial fertilizers and pesticides for the developing world, in an effort to help the poorest countries achieve self-sufficiency. After some initial success in India and Southeast Asia the effects have been disappointing, with only the richest landowners able to afford the supplies and equipment.

In the developing world there is a move toward splitting up the great estates and plantations of the former colonial owners. Such big estates were not very intensively farmed, so sharing the land out among the poorer farmers and landless people, and giving them encouragement and financial incentives to produce subsistence crops, uses the land more productively. This patchwork revolution should achieve more success than the green revolution in reducing world hunger in the 1990s.

HOW DID ANIMAL HUSBANDRY DEVELOP?

Left Transhumance, in which livestock is moved from one area to another in search of fresh pasture at different times of the year, is still practiced in areas such as Iran.

Right top The wild boar is the ancestral animal from which modern pigs have developed. It is a typical forest animal and can live on a wide variety of food. Its versatility made it attractive to early farmers.

Right bottom The wild boar's descendant, one of the hundreds of breeds of domestic pig, is a much larger animal than its ancestor. Large strains have been interbred to produce an animal that will give a high yield of meat.

THE HUNTER-GATHERER way of life depended largely on what kind of animal life was available in an area. Animals were basically hunted and killed for their meat, but other commodities were obtained as well. Skins and hair were used for clothing, dung was used as a fuel, and bones and horns were used for tools and ornaments.

In the tropics, many different types of food animal were available, and it is mostly in tropical areas that the hunter-gatherer way of life still exists today.

PASTORAL NOMADS

In grasslands and tundra areas, there tend to be fewer types of animals but they exist in large herds. In these places, the life of the human group and that of the animal herd become closely linked and so the nomadic way of life evolved.

As herd animals tend to migrate, following the seasons, the tribes that feed on them migrate as well, keeping the animals in sight, so that the herds would be protected if they came under attack from predatory animals. Today, this pastoral nomadic way of life is pursued by the Lapps of Scandinavia who follow the reindeer herds, the Bedouin of Arabia who follow the camels, and the Fulani of Senegal who follow their herds of cattle.

From such a situation it is easy to see how a more settled way of life developed, in which the food animals were penned up so that they were always available. This went hand-in-hand with the development of farming in the Neolithic cultures and the earliest domesticated animals were cows, pigs, camels, and yaks. It was soon appreciated that the great strength of the larger animals could be harnessed and used. So animals were kept as beasts of burden to turn mill wheels, pull ploughs, and carry people about. Dogs also became domesticated and were used to help in hunting and herding.

In the farming technique known as transhumance, practiced mostly in the Alps, the original migratory habits of the animals are still taken into account. Sheep are taken up into the mountain pastures during the summer but brought into the sheltered valleys for the winter.

INTRODUCED ANIMALS

Since most domesticated animals are grassland animals, many of the world's natural grasslands are given over to ranching. The "cowboy" tradition of American nineteenth-century history arose because of the exploitation of the prairies for beef. Likewise, the pampas of South America support a great beef industry, with their own cowboys, the gauchos.

IMPROVING NATURE

Animals change through the course of evolution, and this involves two processes – mutation, in which the genetic make-up of an animal changes; and natural selection, in which this change survives or dies out depending on its suitability for its environment. The breeding of animals for particular purposes has always involved an artificial form of natural selection, so usurping the second part of the evolutionary process. Now, with the advent of genetic engineering, it will soon be able to usurp the first part of the process and introduce the mutation artificially.

It was realized very quickly that the grasslands of Australia would be ideal for sheep and so sheep farming became the greatest industry on that continent.

There have always been dangers in this, however. The introduction of European rabbits to Australia in the nineteenth century as a possible food animal led to widespread devastation of the grasslands. Even now much of the tropical rain forest of South America is being cleared in order to make more grassland to feed more beef cattle, primarily to provide cheap beef for hamburgers.

MODERN ANIMAL HUSBANDRY

For most of history, animal husbandry was an essential part of any farm. However, with the advent of mechanical power, the pack animal has almost disappeared from western agriculture, although animals for meat, milk and wool are still big business. Different types of animal are developed through cross-breeding of animals with particular desirable characteristics. The newly-developing science of genetic engineering may mean that new strains of animals will be developed by direct manipulation of genes in the future.

In modern intensive farming very large numbers of pigs or poultry are kept in a closely controlled artificial environment. The types of livestock are bred for fast growth and high yield of meat or eggs. The animal never leaves the building, food is brought to it, waste is removed, and the stable environment eliminates its natural seasonal growth variations. Such a system is so different from the animal's natural way of life that many regard it with distaste.

WHERE DOES WOOD COME FROM?

LUMBER IS ONE of the most important of raw materials. The first homes of early humans were made from sticks and branches, and when tools were developed, trees were cut down for more substantial structures.

TROPICAL HARDWOODS

The broadleaved, evergreen trees of the tropical rain forests have always been in demand for their high quality wood. The most important of these include mahogany, rosewood, ebony, teak, and greenheart. Extraction has always been difficult due to unhealthy climate, thick undergrowth, poor communications, and scattered, inaccessible stands of particular trees. However, high prices for the product have meant that tropical logging has been a major industry in much of the developed world. This is contributing to the destruction of the world's tropical rain forests, bringing a host of environmental problems. As well as lumber, a properly managed tropical rain forest should yield medicinal plants, oils, spices, gums, beverages, rubber, and animal products.

TEMPERATE HARDWOODS

The temperate hardwoods, like those of the tropical forests, are used for furniture and veneers. The trees exploited include oak, ash, and beech in Europe; quebracho in South America; kari in New Zealand; eucalyptus in Australia; and redwood in California. Species of oak in Mediterranean regions are exploited, not primarily for their lumber, but for their bark from which cork is made.

THE DEMAND FOR TROPICAL WOOD

● It has been predicted that production of tropical hardwoods will double by the end of the century in response to demand from developed countries.

● Uncontrolled logging is extremely wasteful. Only the largest trees are extracted and all other vegetation is destroyed.

● Exporting countries might look after their forests if they obtained better value from them. Establishing management programs would help to save remaining forests.

Above Tropical forests contain many hundreds of different species of tree. They have always been looked upon as a valuable store of different types of wood, each with different properties.

Left Single species forestry, such as this plantation of spruce in northern Scotland, results in vast forests of the same type of tree, all at the same size and stage of development. Whole areas are harvested at once.

TEMPERATE SOFTWOODS

The coniferous trees of the cool regions, such as pine, spruce, and fir, provide the bulk of the world's lumber. The uses of softwoods include lumber for building, wood pulp, newsprint, furniture, and laminated boards. Cellulose is obtained as a by-product and this is an important raw material, being used in the manufacture of alcohol and synthetic fabrics.

Since softwoods grow in uniform stands over wide areas they are more convenient to work than hardwoods. Canada and Scandinavia are major producers of softwoods.

MANAGED FORESTRY

The earliest planned forest was planted in Nuremberg in Germany in 1368. Coppicing was a widespread practice in the Middle Ages when trees such as hazel and chestnut were pruned to the ground every three to twenty years to encourage the prolific growth of thin shoots. The large quantities of branches produced would be harvested for firewood and for fencing.

There are two principal methods of tree-planting. The most basic is the single-species forest, widely used where bare ground is to be turned to commercial use. The trees are grown like an agricultural crop, with seeds of fast-growing trees planted in nurseries and the subsequent seedlings planted out as a forest. This results in straight rows of the same type of tree, all of the same age and size. Often the tree is a foreign species, such as Californian Monterey pine grown in South America and southern Africa, and Australian eucalyptus planted in India.

Criticism of such a system hinges on the loss of the natural habitat over vast areas with the resulting loss of wildlife and native trees. A more acceptable approach is that of selection forestry. The forests are planted with several different types of tree that are native to the area, such as lodgepole pine, Douglas fir, and red pine grown together in Oregon, and at different times. The result is a natural-looking forest in which the trees are harvested individually as they mature.

WHERE ARE FISH CAUGHT?

FISHING BEGAN BACK in the hunter-gatherer stage of human development, among people who lived by the sea or close to rivers. As a food, fish has a similar nutritional content to meat but is generally less fatty. The sea is a vast hunting ground and over the centuries its exploitation has become more and more mechanized and sophisticated.

their ecosystems for drift nets kill dolphins and other creatures not wanted by the fishermen, and trawls plough up the seabed. Long-line fishing, in which individual hooks are baited and deployed, can be used for both pelagic and demersal fish, as in the Newfoundland cod fishery. Seine netting, in which a drift net is pulled into a bag shape, is used mostly in

Left Fish traps rely on the fact that once a fish has found its way into a narrow space it has difficulty in finding its way out again. Crab and lobster traps consist of a net cage with an entrance that is funneled inward. Once the animal is inside, lured there by bait consisting of decomposing fish, it cannot find the narrow entrance again. In larger fish traps, such as the stake nets of river mouths and inshore waters, there is usually a long wall of net that intercepts the fish and guides it into the enclosed part of the trap. The net wall and the trap can be seen in this aerial photograph of fish traps in the Philippines. The nets are all aligned with the current so as to catch the fish as they swim by.

FISHING TECHNIQUES

The fishing industry recognizes two different categories of fish. Pelagic fish live near the surface, and the economic types include herring, mackerel, and pilchards. Demersal fish are those that live near the seabed and include cod, haddock, halibut, flounder, and whiting. Pelagic fish are caught by drift netting in which curtain-like nets are hung in the water from a series of buoys. The herring fisheries of the North Sea and the tuna fisheries of the Pacific use this method. Demersal fish are caught by trawling — dragging a bag-like net along the bottom, as in the Icelandic cod fisheries. Both methods are now having a deleterious effect on

confined areas such as the fjords of British Columbia where it is used to catch salmon. Close to the shore, traps and pots are deployed to catch crabs and lobsters. In the tidal waters of Scandinavia and Scotland stake nets anchored to the mud, and haff nets carried by wading fishermen are used to catch salmon. There are also thriving freshwater fisheries, such as the salmon and sturgeon fisheries in the rivers of the former Soviet Union.

FISHING GROUNDS

Most of the world's fishing is done in the cool waters of the northern hemisphere, particularly

Right The most profitable fish to catch are those that swim in shoals, such as these sardines caught off Portugal. Fish live in shoals as a protection against predators – each individual has less chance of being caught while swimming in a mass. This, however, is no defence against modern fishing. After the shoal has been detected by using sonar or radar techniques, vast numbers of fish may be harvested at once. They may even be lured with electrical charges and chemical baits. Advanced techniques that dispense with the traditional nets are being developed, including a kind of huge vacuum cleaner that sucks up entire shoals from the sea.

where a mixing of warm and cold currents encourages the growth of plankton on which the fish feed. The conditions are most often found over shallow banks or continental shelves. These fishing grounds include the North Sea, the Barents Sea, the Newfoundland Grand Banks, and the seas around Japan. In warmer climates, the ocean currents may cause an upwelling of cold water from the depths, which also gives rise to plankton growth. Such fisheries include those of the Pacific coast of North America and the coast of Peru. However, the coast of Peru is vulnerable to the El Niño effect, in which every few years the deep cold water fails to rise, because of changing wind and current patterns.

FISHING INDUSTRY

Other factors determine the distribution of fisheries. There must be large markets nearby to make the hunt worthwhile. Nowadays that is not so important as factory ships can prepare and freeze the catch immediately. The presence of natural harbors, like the firths of Scotland and fjords of Norway, has had an influence on the history of fishing. Related industries, such as canning, smoking and salting, are found near fishing ports.

Fish farming, in which fish and shellfish are reared in tanks and sheltered waters, has been carried out in Southeast Asia for centuries. It is now becoming important elsewhere. In the 1980s, about one tenth of the world's consumed fish came from fisheries. Carp, salmon, trout, catfish, turbot and shellfish such as mussels, clams, oysters, and shrimp are raised in these conditions.

Whaling was once an important means of exploiting sea life. Now it is recognized that the whale stocks have been severely reduced and the whaling industry has all but ceased.

MARINE WARNINGS

● Commercial fish catches have quadrupled from 20 million tonnes to 92 million tonnes since the end of the World War II. This does not include local subsistence fishing.
● Nearly all fishing takes place within 200 miles (322km) of land – the area most prone to marine pollution and environmental damage.
● Nearly all parts of the world report drastically reduced catches.
● There may only be 500 blue whales left, from an original population of a quarter of a million. Other species show similar declines in numbers.

WHERE ARE THE WORLD'S MINERALS?

TECHNOLOGY TENDS TO be based on the availability and the ability to work raw materials. It is no coincidence that we track the early development of civilization by referring to the materials used at the time. Old and New Stone Ages gave way to the Bronze Age, which in turn gave way to the Iron Age, each reflecting a growing sophistication in the handling of mineral resources.

THE MAIN METAL ORES

Iron ore is the material that immediately comes to mind when talking about economic minerals. There are several different types. The main ones are the oxides, including hematite (Fe_2O_2), magnetite (Fe_3O_4) and limonite ($HFeO_2$). The carbonate siderite ($FeCO_3$) is also important. The chief producers of iron ore are the former USSR, Australia, Brazil, the USA, and China.

Copper ore minerals include native copper (Cu), the oxides cuprite (Cu_3O) and tenorite (CuO), the sulphide chalcopyrite ($CuFeS_2$) and the carbonates malachite ($CuCO_3.Cu(OH)_2$) and azurite ($2CuCO_3.Cu(OH)_2$). The ores tend to contain very little usable copper and so smelting is often done at the mine site to reduce the costs of transportation. The important copper-producing nations are the USA, the former USSR, Chile, Zambia (where the copper producing region is called the Copper Belt), Canada, and Australia.

The main mineral of tin is the oxide cassiterite (SnO_2), and this is mined mostly in Malaysia, Bolivia, Thailand, and Indonesia.

Aluminum is obtained from bauxite which is the hydrated form of the oxide alumina (Al_2O_3). The chief producers are Australia, Jamaica, Guinea, the former USSR, Guyana, and Surinam.

OUT OF REACH – FOR THE MOMENT

The peculiar chemistry of the cold waters of the deep ocean floor means that certain economic metals, such as manganese, iron, nickel and cobalt are deposited as crusts and nodules over vast areas. During the 1970s, much research was done into the economic harvesting of these nodules. However, there will be no exploitation of these until the more accessible land-based reserves become severely depleted.

ORE EMPLACEMENTS

The geology of ore minerals is quite complex and they occur in many different forms. The emplacements, known as veins or lodes, are associated with igneous rocks. Hot fluids seep through the rocks of an area – the country rock – as an intrusive igneous mass cools. These fluids deposit the ore minerals in cracks and fissures both in the country rock and in the igneous body itself. Copper, zinc, lead, and silver ores are found in veins, but the veins are irregular and so can be difficult to work.

Bedded ores are found as sedimentary deposits, as in the salts that are laid down as an inland sea evaporates. Gypsum, potash, and common salt are minerals formed in this way. Bauxite, being formed by alteration of surface rocks, can be regarded as a bedded ore.

Placer deposits (those found on the surface) are formed from particles of heavy ore minerals that have been concentrated by wave action and deposited in layers on a beach. The lighter sand grains are washed away by the sea, leaving the heavy grains behind. Most of the commercially mined tin is extracted from placer ores.

THE MINING INDUSTRY

Many factors influence the exploitation of ores. These include the quality of the ore, the size of the deposit, and the value of any secondary minerals. Economic factors include the market demand, the labour supply, the transport costs, the capital available, and any political or strategic considerations. A trade embargo on a mineral-producing nation may cause a previously uneconomic reserve of that mineral in another nation to become worth exploiting.

OTHER MINERAL RESOURCES

Ores are not the only minerals worth exploiting. Bulk minerals include building stone, clay, sand, gravel, slate, and other materials used in the building industry. Because of their bulk they tend to be exploited close to their markets.

Chemical raw materials include salt, potash, sulphur, nitrate, gypsum, and other materials that are used in the chemical industry.

Left The intense mountain-building activity and vulcanism along the Andes has led to the emplacement of many valuable ores, such as those exploited by this copper foundry at Chuquicamata in Chile.

Below The biggest hole in Europe is the Penrhyn slate quarry in north Wales. It was opened in 1765 and yields red, blue, and green slate of the highest quality. Slate is used for roofing and billiard tables.

THIN PICKINGS

Geologists recognize about 2,000 different minerals that form the Earth's crust. Of these, only about 100 are of economic importance.

WHAT SUPPLIES CIVILIZATION'S POWER?

THE EARLIEST FORMS of power used by civilization came from pack animals and beasts of burden. Then natural forces of wind and water currents were harnessed to turn mills for grinding corn, and for driving ships along.

COAL

The Industrial Revolution of eighteenth-century Europe was largely driven by coal. Coal is formed by the partial decomposition of plant matter, in which the oxygen is lost and the carbon content is concentrated. Most commercial coal deposits date from the Carboniferous period.

There are many grades of coal. The first stage of its formation is the production of peat — a soft fibrous substance. This is exploited in Ireland, but nowadays as a horticultural medium rather than as a source of power. A greater concentration of carbon gives lignite, or brown coal. Lignite beds dating from the Tertiary are exploited in Germany and Poland. The next stage is bituminous coal, which comprises the greatest proportion of coal extracted throughout the world. If the coal beds are subjected to great heat and pressure in the Earth they produce the highest grade of all — anthracite. Wales is famous for its anthracite beds.

A RAPID RETURN

The formation of the world's coal supply involved the extraction of vast quantities of carbon dioxide from the atmosphere by growing plants. This process took millions upon millions of years. Now that we are burning the coal we are returning that carbon dioxide to the atmosphere – many millions of years' worth of carbon dioxide in a few decades. This may drastically affect both the atmosphere and the climate of our world.

OIL

Organic matter deposited and buried on an oxygen-poor seabed may retain its carbon in the form of oil droplets. Eventually, the sediments containing the oil droplets will turn to rock and, if the rock is porous enough, the droplets will float upward through the water contained in the pores. If the droplets meet a covering of impermeable rock they will build up into a petroleum reservoir. This is the geological basis for the modern oil industry. The conditions were first recognized in Pennsylvania and along the Californian coast, but nowadays most oil is obtained from the Arabian Gulf, the Gulf of Mexico, the former USSR, and the North Sea.

Left The conventional coal mine is a system of tunnels driven along an underground seam. Where a seam is near the surface it may be exploited by open-cast or strip mining. The overburden of soil and rock are removed, the coal taken out, and the overburden replaced, as in this lignite mine in Wyoming.

Right opposite Volcanic water heated underground cannot be utilized directly because of the chemicals in it. Instead, it is pumped to heat exchangers where the heat is transferred to domestic and industrial water supplies or used to generate electricity. This example is in Wairakei in New Zealand.

GAS

Natural gas, consisting largely of methane, ethane, butane, and propane, accumulates in natural traps like those of petroleum. It is formed by the breakdown of oil or coal, and so tends to be found in areas where oil or coal already occur, such as the North sea.

HYDROELECTRIC POWER

The old technique of letting natural water currents turn a wheel is updated in hydroelectric power generation, in which water falling from a reservoir turns turbines that drive electricity generators. Mountainous areas and reliable rainfall are needed to produce the constant head of water, as are solid rocky foundations for the installations. Scandinavia, Switzerland, and the USA are major producers of hydroelectric power.

Tidal power uses similar techniques, but with the ebb and flow of the tide. It is currently being exploited to a great extent only in France.

NUCLEAR POWER

Nuclear energy uses the energy released as atoms split. By 1990 there were 424 nuclear power stations throughout the world. General distrust of the tech-nology and the safety factors, especially in the light of many nuclear accidents in the former USSR that only became known in 1991, means that this will always be a controversial source of energy. Some nations, for example New Zealand, have a stated anti-nuclear policy.

A possible future development may be nuclear fusion (as opposed to nuclear fission) in which energy is released as atoms combine. This would have the advantage of unlimited fuel (hydrogen from seawater), few dangerous products and greater safety.

GEOTHERMAL ENERGY

In volcanic areas, the heat of the magma beneath the Earth's surface can be tapped and used for power generation. This is necessarily restricted to volcanic areas such as Iceland, New Zealand, and Italy.

RENEWABLE RESOURCES

An energy resource that can be replaced by natural processes is termed a renewable resource. The term covers solar power, wave energy, natural gas from the decomposition of rubbish and animal wastes, and hydroelectric power. Apart from hydroelectric power, the potential of renewable resources has still to be developed fully.

WHAT INFLUENCES SETTLEMENT?

SOME PEOPLE LIVE in scattered groups, some in villages, some in towns, some in cities. The reasons for the developments of the various places are numerous.

VILLAGES

The original sites of settlements tended to be due to good agricultural possibilities. Springline settlements were established along hillsides where fresh water was always available. Flood-plain settlements were built along the sides of river valleys, where the valley itself provided good agricultural soil but the

village was located far enough from the river to avoid flooding.

Other settlements depended on trade. An obvious place for a settlement would be where it was easy to cross a river, so all the local traffic would pass through. The highest navigation point on a river was also a good site. Villages grew up where main trade routes crossed.

In times of strife, settlements would be built on hilltops or other defensible positions.

PORTS

Settlements by the sea have their own factors that contribute to their growth and survival. The main factor is the presence of a sheltered anchorage and deep water giving unrestricted access for the ships. They may be fishing ports if they are close enough to good fishing grounds. Commercial ports develop close to industrial areas or production centers of raw materials. The port may develop its own storage and distribution system for the goods imported. Such a port is called entrepôt. A packet station is a port that deals with passengers and mail. Naval ports are situated close to strategic waterways.

TOWNS

As the most successful villages grew into towns and cities their function often changed. Some became administrative centers for larger areas.

With the coming of industrialization, some villages grew into manufacturing centers because the trade routes that passed through them brought a particular raw material. For example, coal and iron found in the same region would give rise to iron and steel industries.

Above Rotterdam in the Netherlands is a typical industrial port. Situated at the mouths of the Rhine and the Maas it is in a good position to handle the goods passing up and down these rivers. It became the hub of a European canal system in the late nineteenth century.

TOWNS WITH SPECIFIC FUNCTIONS

Administrative center	Brazilia, New Delhi
Manufacturing center	Pittsburg, Sheffield
Religious center	Lourdes, Mecca
Service town	Zurich, Cambridge
Commuter town	Dorking, Jersey City
Tourist center	Zermatt, Cape Cod
New town	Vallingby, Welwyn

Some towns developed as religious centers, being associated with some famous figure or event from a religious tradition.

A town may happen to develop a reputation for some particular service, such as banking, and subsequent generations of the business thrive there because of the tradition.

As cities grew in size, surrounding towns became dormitory towns, being the living areas of the city working population.

With the growth of the leisure industries in the nineteenth and twentieth centuries, towns that were sited by the sea, or in some picturesque place, became holiday resorts and tourist centers.

As populations burgeoned in the mid-twentieth century, new towns were planned and built. In most cases these were designed with a complete community in mind — central business and shopping areas integrated with residential districts, industrial areas and open spaces and parks.

In highly industrialized countries, a town that originally developed at a major route center may now have the through traffic diverted away in a bypass, so extinguishing the original purpose of that town's existence.

COMMUNICATIONS

The change in a settlement's main function is often due to the change in communications. Britain and Europe once had extensive systems of canals, pro-

Below Desert towns owe their existence to the presence of an oasis or a route center. Agadez, in the Republic of Niger, is situated at the crossroads of a number of routes across the Sahara desert. The produce of the surrounding lands, including dates and salt, is for sale in the market place, traded from the passing caravans.

TOWN SITES

Springline settlement	Denver, Turin
Flood-plain settlement	Bologna, Nîmes
Bridging point	Paris, London
Defensible position	Edinburgh, Quebec

PORTS

Fishing port	New Bedford
Commercial port	Rotterdam
Packet station	Dover
Naval port	Vladivostok

viding cheap but slow transportation of goods between manufacturer and consumer; and towns grew up along the canal banks. However, the canals were subsequently superseded by the railways, and then by the road networks. The development of the railway system in the United States following the Civil War opened up areas of the plains to livestock breeding and afforded easy communications between the east and west coasts. The importance of the railways has now been largely replaced by the network of roads and the domestic airline system.

Ocean shipping has always been important, with different sized and equipped ships dealing with different commodities. Strife in the Middle East and the vulnerability of the Suez Canal led to the development of supertankers for transporting petroleum in bulk. The late twentieth century saw the development of container ships designed to simplify the handling of diverse cargoes.

Air transport is a twentieth-century invention, and has now taken over from sea transport in the carriage of passengers and mail.

WORLD GAZETTEER

1 Canada
2 The United States
3 Belize
4 Costa Rica
5 El Salvador
6 Guatemala
7 Honduras
8 Nicaragua
9 Panama
10 Mexico
11 Barbados
12 Bahamas
13 Dominica
14 Dominican Republic
15 Grenada
16 Jamaica
17 Cuba
18 Haiti
19 Trinidad and Tobago
20 St. Lucia
21 St. Vincent and the Grenadines
22 Antigua and Barbuda
23 Anguilla
24 Cayman Islands
25 Guadeloupe
26 Martinique
27 Montserrat
28 Puerto Rico
29 Turks and Caicos Islands
30 Virgin Islands
31 Guyana
32 French Guiana
33 Brazil
34 Bolivia
35 Colombia
36 Ecuador
37 Peru
38 Surinam
39 Venezuela
40 Uruguay
41 Argentina
42 Chile
43 Paraguay
44 Egypt
45 Algeria
46 Sudan
47 Libya
48 Mauritania
49 Morocco
50 Ethiopia
51 Chad
52 Djibouti
53 Mali
54 Niger
55 Western Sahara
56 Tunisia
57 Central African Republic
58 São Tomé and Principe
59 Nigeria
60 Gabon
61 Burkina Faso
62 Benin
63 Congo
64 Cameroon
65 Cape Verde
66 Equatorial Guinea
67 The Gambia
68 Ghana
69 Guinea
70 Guinea-Bissau
71 Ivory Coast
72 Liberia
73 Senegal
74 Sierra Leone
75 Togo
76 Zaïre

77 Madagascar
78 Réunion
79 Comoros
80 Burundi
81 Kenya
82 Rwanda
83 Seychelles
84 Uganda
85 Somalia
86 Mauritius
87 Tanzania
88 Lesotho
89 Swaziland
90 Namibia
91 Angola
92 Mozambique
93 Botswana
94 Malawi
95 South Africa
96 Zambia
97 Zimbabwe
98 Cyprus
99 Jordan
100 Iran
101 Saudi Arabia
102 Iraq
103 Lebanon
104 Turkey
105 Yemen
106 Oman
107 Bahrain
108 Israel
109 Kuwait
110 Qatar
111 Syria
112 United Arab Emirates
113 Sri Lanka
114 Pakistan
115 Brunei
116 Bhutan
117 Thailand
118 Laos
119 Malaysia
120 Nepal
121 Bangladesh
122 Afghanistan
123 India
124 Indonesia
125 Philippines
126 Singapore
127 Vietnam
128 Cambodia
129 Myanmar
130 North Korea
131 Hong Kong
132 Japan
133 Macau
134 Mongolia
135 China
136 Taiwan
137 South Korea
138 Armenia
139 Azerbaijan
140 Belarus
141 Estonia
142 Georgia
143 Kazakhstan
144 Kyrgyzstan
145 Latvia
146 Lithuania
147 Moldova
148 The Russian Federation
149 Tajikistan
150 Turkmenistan
151 Ukraine
152 Uzbekistan

153 Greenland
154 Denmark
155 Norway
156 Sweden
157 Finland
158 Iceland
159 Republic of Ireland
160 United Kingdom
161 Germany
162 France
163 Luxembourg
164 Belgium
165 Netherlands
166 Monaco
167 Liechtenstein
168 Austria
169 Italy
170 Malta
171 San Marino
172 Switzerland
173 Vatican City
174 Gibraltar
175 Andorra
176 Portugal
177 Spain
178 Czechoslovakia
179 Greece
180 Bulgaria
181 Albania
182 Hungary
183 Poland
184 Romania
185 Yugoslavia
186 Australia
187 American Samoa
188 Cook Islands
189 French Polynesia
190 Western Samoa
191 Tonga
192 New Caledonia
193 New Zealand
194 Papua New Guinea
195 Fiji
196 Kiribati
197 Nauru
198 Vanuatu
199 Solomon Islands
200 Tuvalu

World • Political

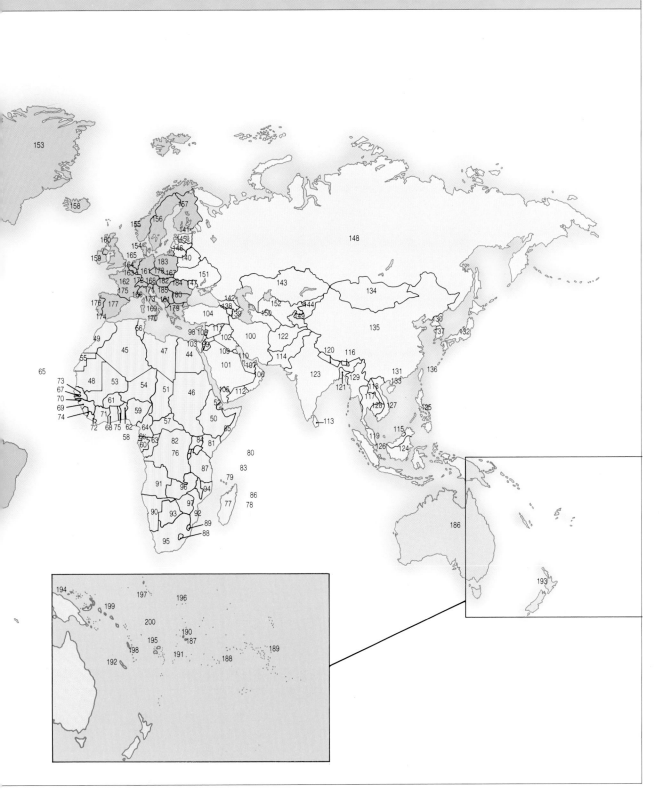

WORLD GAZETTEER

World • Physical

World • Vegetation

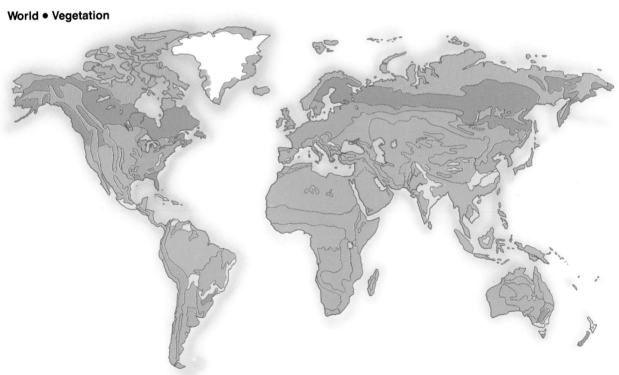

World • Population

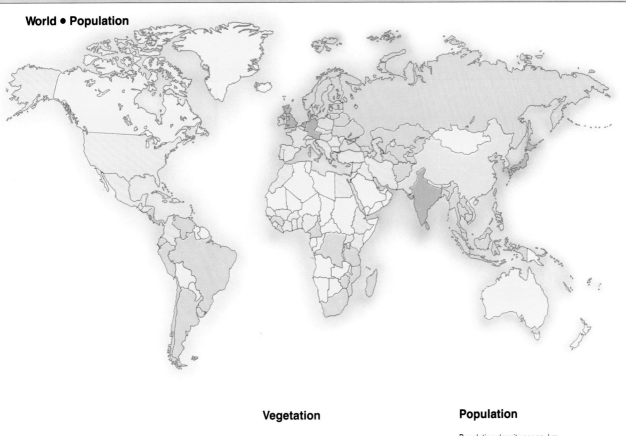

Vegetation

- ice
- mountain vegetation
  tundra
- boreal forest
  conifer forest
- mixed forest
  broadleaf forest
- tropical rainforest
  monsoon forest
- dry-tropical forest
  sub-tropical forest
- Mediterranean scrub
  prairie
  steppe
  savanna
- dry-tropical scrub and thorn forest
  desert

Population

Population density per sq. km.
- less than 10 inhabitants
- 10–25 inhabitants
- 25–100 inhabitants
- 100–200 inhabitants
- over 200 inhabitants

NORTH AMERICA

Area: (including Central America and Greenland) 9,420,000 sq miles (24,398,000km²)

Highest point: Mount McKinley, Alaska, 20,320ft (6,194m)

Lowest point: Death Valley, California, 282ft (86m) below sea level

NORTH AMERICA IS the landmass that occupies the northern part of the western hemisphere. It has the classic continental structure of a flat core of ancient metamorphic rocks, partially covered by later sedimentary rocks, and surrounded by progressively younger fold mountain chains. The metamorphic core is the Canadian Shield which contains some of the oldest rocks known, and which is partially flooded by Hudson's Bay. Toward the south, the shield is covered by younger sedimentary rocks forming the prairies and plains of the central continent. In the east, lie the Appalachian mountain chains, formed between the Devonian and Permian periods, 400-250 million years ago. In the west, lie the Rocky Mountains that began forming in late Carboniferous times. A series of younger ranges, the Coast Range, the Cascade Range, and the Sierra Nevada, have since developed along the western seaboard. The mountains along here are still active, as shown by the number of volcanoes, including Mount Saint Helens, and the frequency of earthquakes, particularly along the San Andreas Fault. The whole complex of western mountains has formed the isthmus of Central America and connected North America to the South American continent in geologically recent times. It has also intermittently formed a land bridge to northern Asia.

The inland plains are drained by a complex of rivers which eventually flow southward to the Gulf of Mexico as the Mississippi. On the Canadian Shield itself most of the landscape features have been generated by the movement of glaciers during the Ice Age. Many lakes occupy the hollows so formed. The Great Lakes, which include some of the largest freshwater lakes in the world, lie at the southern edge of the Shield and are drained to the Atlantic ocean by the St. Lawrence River.

Climates range from tropical rain forest conditions in Central America to polar and tundra conditions in the far north. In between lie tropical deserts, continental climates, Mediterranean climates, and maritime climates.

Left The Colorado River's Grand Canyon was made a national park in 1919. It is 217 miles (350 km) long and over a mile (1.6 km) deep.

The first people to populate the continent were probably hunter-gatherers who crossed from Asia during the last great cold spell of the Ice Age some time between 30,000 and 19,000 years ago. Most of the north of the continent east of the Rocky Mountains was ice and snow at that time. However, the offshore islands and many of the deep mountain valleys, such as those of Yukon and Mackenzie, were probably ice-free and could be used for migration. These peoples were the ancestors of the modern Native Americans. A second migration took place some time between 10,000 and 8,000 years ago, bringing a different group of coastal hunter-gatherers along the Aleutian islands. These were the ancestors of the modern Inuit, or Eskimo, and they had spread across the Canadian Arctic to Greenland by 4,000 years ago.

European settlers began arriving in the fifteenth century, mostly from Spain, although there is a possibility that people from Scandinavia visited the continent several centuries before this. The Native Americans and the Inuit have now been all but supplanted by peoples from all over the world.

Top The Rocky Mountains provide the backbone of North America. To the east lie the Great Plains, and to the west lie the Coast Ranges, the Cascades and the Pacific ocean.

Above The vast distances and the sprawling cities of North America mean that most families aspire to owning at least one car for the sake of mobility.

CANADA

Above Montreal in Quebec is, apart
from Paris, the world's largest French-
speaking city. It lies at the confluence of
the Ottawa River and St. Lawrence
Seaway and as such it is an important
inland port.

Far right Lake Louise in British
Columbia is one of about 80 lakes that
lie in the Canadian Rockies and Coast
Ranges of that province. This is the
most westerly and most mountainous
of the provinces of Canada.

CANADA IS BOUNDED to the south by
the main part of the USA with
much of the boundary lying along the
latitude of 49°N – the forty-ninth
parallel. To the northwest it adjoins
the American state of Alaska. Its
nearest neighbor to the northeast
is Greenland, a Danish possession.

The land
Most of the low-lying land of Canada
is the Canadian Shield, a vast
expanse of ancient metamorphic
rocks. The natural vegetation here
is largely coniferous forest with
temperate grassland in the south
and tundra in the far north. Lakes
formed in hollows produced by ice
caps during the Ice Age lie across
the Shield. The largest of these are
the Great Lakes in the south, and
Lake Winnipeg, Great Slave Lake,
and Great Bear Lake further north.
To the west lie the Rocky Mountains
and the Coast Ranges. In the far
north, the continent breaks up into
many islands, the largest of which
are Baffin, Victoria, and Ellesmere
islands. These islands are ice-
bound for most of the year.

The people
Canada is the second largest country
in the world. Even so its population
is very small. The Native Americans
and the Inuit were the original
inhabitants. French and British
settlers began to come in the
seventeenth century. In 1867, it
gained its independence from the

British Empire and in 1982 the British government ceased to have any legal control over Canadian affairs, although it is still a member of the Commonwealth. The French influence has always been strong, especially in Quebec, and from time to time there are demands for Quebec to become an independent French-speaking nation. More than half of the population lives around the Great Lakes and the St. Lawrence in the southeast.

Canada is an important manufacturing nation. Like the population, most of the industry is concentrated in the southeastern corner. Agriculture is also important, but the hostile nature of much of the terrain means that only about 7 per cent of the land is cultivated. About two-thirds of Canada's trade is with the USA.

PROVINCES OF CANADA

Province	Area sq miles (km²)	Population	Capital
Alberta (1)	255,287 (661,190)	2,375,000	Edmonton
British Columbia (2)	366,255 (948,595)	2,889,000	Victoria
Manitoba (3)	251,002 (650,090)	1,071,000	Winnipeg
New Brunswick (4)	28,353 (73,435)	710,000	Fredericton
Newfoundland (5)	156,186 (404,520)	568,000	St John's
Northwest Territories (6)	1,304,906 (3,379,685)	52,000	Yellowknife
Nova Scotia (7)	21,424 (55,490)	873,000	Halifax
Ontario (8)	412,601 (1,068,630)	9,114,000	Toronto
Prince Edward Island (9)	2,183 (5,655)	127,000	Charlottetown
Quebec (10)	594,861 (1,540,690)	6,540,000	Quebec
Saskatchewan (11)	251,635 (651,700)	1,010,000	Regina
Yukon Territory (12)	186,250 (482,515)	24,000	Whitehorse

THE UNITED STATES

KEY FACTS

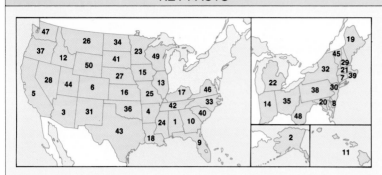

Official name: United States of America

Area: 3,618,770 sq miles (9,368,900km²)

Population: 250,372,000, of whom 26,500,000 are black, 20,000,000 Hispanic and 1,000,000 Native Americans

Capital: Washington DC

Languages: English, Spanish

Main exports: wheat, farm produce, machinery

Currency: US dollar

THE MAIN PART of the United States of America occupies the southern half of the North American continent, bounded to the north along the forty-ninth parallel by Canada, and to the south by Mexico. The state of Alaska lies in the northwest corner of the continent and also occupies a strip of the Pacific coastline. The state of Hawaii consists of a chain of volcanic islands in the Pacific Ocean and situated close to the Tropic of Cancer.

The land

The eastern section of mainland USA consists of the old Appalachian mountains and the

coastal strip. In the center are the low-lying prairies drained by the Mississippi river system. To the west rise the Rocky Mountains, and the Cascade Mountains and Sierra Nevada close to the west coast.

The people

The United States of America has always been regarded as the melting pot of the world – a place where people of all nationalities could settle and become a single nation. The original inhabitants, the Native Americans or "Indians," occupied the land about 20,000 years ago. Now their numbers are greatly reduced and about half of them are concentrated in Arizona, California, New Mexico, North Carolina, and Oklahoma. During the last 500 years, settlers came from Europe, especially Britain, Italy, and Ireland and settled predominantly on the east coast. French settlers spread northwards along the Mississippi. Spanish people moved up the west coast from Central and South America. Africans were brought to the south-eastern states as slaves for the cotton plantations and this has given rise to the large black population in this area. The Chinese communities of the west coast originated as cheap labor brought over to help construct the railway system.

Above left The USA's technology is shown by the space program. Although not the first into space, the USA is the only nation to put a man on the moon and to develop a space shuttle.

Left New York harbor, with the Statue of Liberty, built to commemorate the centenary of independence, was traditionally the first sight that European settlers had of their New World.

STATES OF THE USA			
State	**Area sq miles (km²)**	**Population**	**Capital**
Alabama (1)	50,766 (131,485)	4,021,000	Montgomery
Alaska (2)	570,833 (1,478,450)	521,000	Juneau
Arizona (3)	113,508 (293,835)	3,489,000	Phoenix
Arkansas (4)	52,077 (134,880)	2,359,000	Little Rock
California (5)	156,300 (404,815)	28,314,000	Sacramento
Colorado (6)	103,595 (268,310)	3,303,000	Denver
Connecticut (7)	4,872 (12,620)	3,174,000	Hartford
Delaware (8)	1,932 (5,005)	622,000	Dover
Florida (9)	54,152 (140,255)	11,366,000	Tallahassee
Georgia (10)	58,056 (150,365)	5,976,000	Atlanta
Hawaii (11)	6,425 (16,640)	1,098,000	Honolulu
Idaho (12)	82,415 (213,455)	1,003,000	Boise
Illinois (13)	55,645 (144,120)	11,535,000	Springfield
Indiana (14)	35,932 (93,065)	5,499,000	Indianapolis
Iowa (15)	55,965 (144,950)	2,884,000	Des Moines
Kansas (16)	81,778 (211,805)	2,495,000	Topeka
Kentucky (17)	39,668 (102,740)	3,679,000	Frankfort
Louisiana (18)	44,521 (115,310)	4,481,000	Baton Rouge
Maine (19)	30,994 (80,275)	1,164,000	Augusta
Maryland (20)	9,837 (25,480)	4,392,000	Annapolis
Massachusetts (21)	7,824 (20,265)	5,822,000	Boston
Michigan (22)	56,957 (147,520)	9,088,000	Lansing
Minnesota (23)	79,548 (206,030)	4,193,000	St. Paul
Mississippi (24)	47,233 (122,335)	2,613,000	Jackson
Missouri (25)	68,944 (178,565)	5,029,000	Jefferson City
Montana (26)	145,389 (376,555)	805,000	Helena
Nebraska (27)	76,643 (198,505)	1,602,000	Lincoln
Nevada (28)	113,755 (294,624)	1,054,000	Carson City
New Hampshire (29)	8,992 (23,290)	998,000	Concord
New Jersey (30)	7,467 (19,340)	7,562,000	Trenton
New Mexico (31)	121,334 (314,255)	1,507,000	Santa Fe
New York (32)	47,376 (122,705)	17,783,000	Albany
North Carolina (33)	48,843 (126,505)	6,255,000	Raleigh
North Dakota (34)	69,300 (179,485)	667,000	Bismarck
Ohio (35)	41,000 (106,200)	10,744,000	Columbus
Oklahoma (36)	68,635 (177,815)	3,242,000	Oklahoma City
Oregon (37)	96,184 (249,115)	2,767,000	Salem
Pennsylvania (38)	44,888 (116,260)	11,852,000	Harrisburg
Rhode Island (39)	1,054 (2,730)	968,000	Providence
South Carolina (40)	30,200 (78,225)	3,347,000	Columbia
South Dakota (41)	75,952 (196,715)	713,000	Pierre
Tennessee (42)	41,154 (106,590)	4,762,000	Nashville
Texas (43)	262,017 (678,620)	16,370,000	Austin
Utah (44)	82,074 (212,570)	1,690,000	Salt Lake City
Vermont (45)	9,613 (24,900)	535,000	Montpelier
Virginia (46)	39,695 (102,835)	5,387,000	Richmond
Washington (47)	66,512 (172,265)	4,648,000	Olympia
Washington DC	63 (163)	626,000	Washington DC
West Virginia (48)	24,119 (62,470)	1,936,000	Charleston
Wisconsin (49)	24,119 (140,965)	4,775,000	Madison
Wyoming (50)	66,512 (251,200)	479,000	Cheyenne

CENTRAL AMERICA

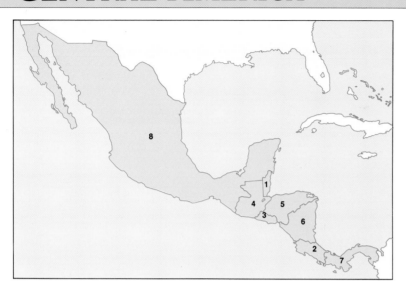

CENTRAL AMERICA IS the isthmus that joins the continents of North America and South America. It can be thought of as part of the mountain range that runs continuously down the western portions of the two continents. The narrowest part of the region lies in Panama where it is the site of the Panama Canal.

The land
Central America is quite recent in geological origin. Until about two million years ago, North and South America were isolated from one another. The region is still active, as is seen by the many active volcanoes, such as El Chichon in the Yucatan, the eruption of which in 1982 led to worldwide climatic

changes. There are many earthquakes too, such as that which shook Mexico City in 1985. The volcanic soil and the hot damp climates of the coastal regions provide good growing conditions for tropical fruits.

Contrasting with these good growing conditions, the Mexican desert spreads across the widest part of the isthmus, lying in the northern tropical desert belt of the world's climates.

The people
Central America had a thriving civilization of such peoples as the Aztecs, Toltecs, and Mixtecs when the Spanish arrived in the sixteenth century. The search for gold brought many people from Europe and the native peoples were wiped out. The modern population is largely of Spanish descent.

The region was part of the Spanish empire until the early 1880s when the empire collapsed and the various nations gained independence, forming the Central American Federation. The close proximity of the USA meant that the area was heavily dependent on that country for trade, giving rise to a strong landowning class that controlled the cash crops.

Left The people of modern Central America are a result of the marriage of the Spanish invaders and the native peoples over the last 500 years. Many of the native traditions are still alive, shown by the colorful clothes and craftware on sale at a market.

Right The ancient Central American peoples, such as the Maya, had very sophisticated civilizations, as seen by their architecture. Chichen Itza was the Maya capital, built in the jungles of the Yucatan – a peninsula on the Caribbean coast of Mexico.

KEY FACTS					
Official name (Capital)	Area sq miles (km²)	Population	Language	Main exports	Currency
Belize (1) (Belmopan)	8,864 (22,963)	180,000	English (official), Spanish	fruit, sugar	Belize dollar
Republic of Costa Rica (2) (San José)	19,735 (51,100)	3,032,000	Spanish	bananas, beef, cocoa, coffee, sugar	colon
Republic of El Salvador (3) (San Salvador)	8,258 (21,393)	5,900,000	Spanish, Nahua	coffee, cotton, sugar	colon
Republic of Guatemala (4) (Guatemala City)	42,031 (108,889)	9,340,000	Spanish, over half speak local languages	bananas, coffee, cotton	quetzal
Republic of Honduras (5) (Tegucigalpa)	43,282 (112,000)	5,106,000	Spanish	coffee, fruit, lumber	lempira
Republic of Nicaragua (6) (Managua)	49,363 (127,849)	3,606,000	Spanish, English	bananas, coffee, cotton, sugar	cordoba
Republic of Panama (7) (Panama City)	29,768 (77,100)	2,423,000	Spanish, English	bananas, copper, petroleum products, shellfish, sugar	balboa
United States of Mexico (8) (Mexico City)	756,198 (1,958,201)	88,335,000	Spanish, some local languages	fruits, handicrafts, metals, vegetables	peso

WEST INDIES

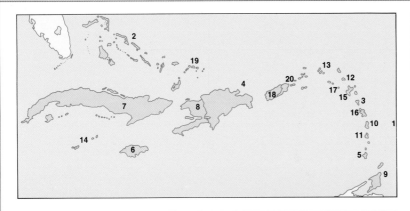

Below White beach, palm trees, blue ocean – the idyllic picture of the West Indies as exploited by the tourist industry. Tourism is becoming a large source of income for the region.

Right Local fisheries thrive on the fishing grounds surrounding the islands. Here, on Martinique, shoals of fish are caught close to shore by using vertical seine nets.

The people

The many local peoples of the islands were displaced by the Spanish colonists in the early 1500s. Slaves were brought to the West Indies from Africa to work the cotton plantations, and the majority of the modern population consists of their descendants.

The mild climates mean that the Caribbean area is developing as a tourist region, and the affluence of the tourists often contrasts starkly with the poverty and overcrowding of the West Indian islands.

THE WEST INDIES is a typical volcanic arc of islands, close to a destructive plate margin. It is an archipelago of about 1,200 islands dividing the Caribbean and the Gulf of Mexico from the Atlantic.

The islands can be divided into three geographic (as opposed to political) groups. The Greater Antilles consists of the bigger islands of Cuba, Hispaniola (Haiti and the Dominican Republic), Jamaica, and Puerto Rico. The Lesser Antilles consists of the string of smaller islands that sweep southward to the Venezuelan coast. The Bahamas is the scatter of low islands between the island arc proper and Florida on the North American mainland.

The land

Like neighboring Central America, the region is geologically quite young and still active. Volcanic activity is frequent, one of the classic volcanic disasters having taken place on the island of Martinique when Mont Pelée exploded in 1902 killing 30,000.

Tropical fruits and cotton grow well because of the rich volcanic soil and the hot damp climates.

The whole area suffers repeatedly from hurricanes because it lies within the hurricane belt.

WEST INDIES DEPENDENCIES	
Island	**Colonial Power**
Anguilla (13)	United Kingdom
Cayman (14)	United Kingdom
Guadeloupe (15)	France
Martinique (16)	France
Montserrat (17)	United Kingdom
Puerto Rico (18)	United States
Turks & Caicos Islands (19)	United Kingdom
Virgin Islands (20)	United States/ United Kingdom

KEY FACTS					
Official name (Capital)	Area sq miles (km²)	Population	Language	Main exports	Currency
Barbados (1) (Bridgetown)	166 (430)	260,000	English	clothing, electronic parts, rum, sugar	Barbados dollar
Commonwealth of the Bahamas (2) (Nassau)	5,352 (13,864)	251,000	English	cement, petroleum products, tourism	Bahamian dollar
Commonwealth of Dominica (3) (Roseau)	290 (751)	94,200	English	fruit	Eastern Caribbean dollar
Dominican Republic (4) (Santo Domingo)	18,700 (48,442)	7,307,000	Spanish	bauxite, coffee, gold, silver, sugar, tobacco	peso
Grenada (5) (St. George's)	131 (340)	84,000	English, some French	bananas, cocoa, spices	Eastern Caribbean dollar
Jamaica (6) (Kingston)	4,230 (10,957)	2,513,000	English, Creole	bauxite, cigars, coconuts, coffee, fruit, liqueurs, rum, sugar	Jamaican dollar
Republic of Cuba (7) (Havana)	42,820 (110,860)	10,582,000	Spanish	coffee, metals, sugar, tobacco	Cuban peso
Republic of Haiti (8) (Port-au-Prince)	10,712 (27,750)	6,409,000	French, Creole	cocoa, coffee, cotton, rice, sisal, sugar	gourde
Republic of Trinidad (9) and Tobago (Port-of-Spain)	Trinidad: 1,864 (4,828) Tobago: 116 (300)	1,270,000	English (official), French, Hindi, Spanish	cocoa, oil, petroleum products, sugar	Trinidad and Tobago dollar
St. Lucia (10) (Castries)	238 (617)	153,000	English, French patois	bananas, cocoa, coconut products	Eastern Caribbean dollar
St. Vincent and the Grenadines (11) (Kingstown)	150 (388)	106,000	English, French patois	arrowroot, bananas, copra, sweet potatoes, taros	Eastern Caribbean dollar
State of Antigua and Barbuda (12) (St. John's)	Antigua: 108 (280) Barbuda: 62 (161)	83,500	English	rum, sea-island cotton, shellfish	Eastern Caribbean dollar

103

SOUTH AMERICA

KEY FACTS

Area: 6,900,000 sq miles (17,864,000km²)

Highest point: Aconcagua, Argentina 22,834ft (6,960m)

World's wettest place: Tutunendo, Colombia 463.4in (11,770mm) of rainfall per year

World's driest place: Atacama desert, Chile, average rainfall nil. Rain fell briefly in 1971 for the first time in 400 years.

SOUTH AMERICA IS the landmass that straddles the equator in the western hemisphere and extends southward almost to the Antarctic Circle. The narrow southern portion sweeps eastward at the tip, and the plate boundary here can be traced into the Atlantic Ocean by the island groups of South Georgia and the South Sandwich islands. The Falkland Islands lie on South America's only broad area of continental shelf in this south-eastern corner. The remarkable thing about the shape of the continent is its east coast. It forms an almost perfect jigsaw fit with the west coast of Africa, providing

Above Macaws are typical of the exotic bird life found in the rain forests of South America.

Right The mighty Amazon river has its source in the deep gorges of the Andes.

one of the proofs that the two were once joined together to form part of a larger supercontinent.

Ancient metamorphic continental blocks are found in the Brazilian Highlands in the east and the Guyana Highlands in the northeast. There they form uplifted plains at an altitude of 2,000-5,000ft (610-1,520m). The vast range of the Andes forms the western section of the continent, running its entire 4,500 mile (7,200km) length. At its widest, in Bolivia, this mountain belt is 400 miles (640km) wide. The range is still active, being shaken periodically by earthquakes and suffering almost continuous volcanic eruptions. The Patagonian plateau in southern Argentina consists of a series of uplands that rise from the Atlantic coast to the foothills of the Andes.

There are three principal lowland areas. The Orinoco river plain lies between the Guyana Highlands and the northernmost part of the Andes. The Amazon basin stretches 2,000 miles (3,200km) from the foothills of the Andes in the west, between the Guyana and Brazil Highlands, to the Atlantic Ocean in the east. The Pampa-Chaco plain of Argentina, Paraguay, and Bolivia is floored with sedimentary rocks formed from debris worn from the Andes and the Brazilian Highlands.

The lowland areas contain very large rivers. The Amazon is one of the longest in the world – 4,000 miles (6,437km). Further south the Parana, Paraguay, and Uruguay unite and flow into the Atlantic as the vast estuary of the River Plate.

The climates and vegetation zones include tropical rainforest along the equator, and grasslands in the river plains and uplands of the south.

The first people reached South America some 20,000 years ago. They were the same people who gave rise to the Native North Americans, and may have spread into the continent by island-hopping along the Caribbean islands or by spreading along the isthmus of Central America. Their direct descendants still exist as hunter-gatherers in the depths of the rain forests. At the end of the fifteenth century, the Europeans began to arrive and until the beginning of the nineteenth century the countries of South America were parts of the Spanish and Portuguese empires.

NORTHERN SOUTH AMERICA

Right Beef farming is important to the South American economy. As a result, large areas of forest are being cleared for extra grazing land.

Below Lake Titicaca, 12,500ft (3,810m) above sea level, lies between Peru and Bolivia and is the largest lake in South America.

THE NORTHERN PART of South America is the broad tropical part. It is the area of the vast Amazon basin, the rain forest of which covers an area larger than Western Europe. The presence of the Andes in the far west means that the drainage of the whole area is toward the east.

The whole of northern South America lies within the tropics, and so the climate is that of the tropical rainforest zone, or the tropical grassland zone. In the west, the Andes modifies this somewhat, there being ice-covered peaks almost on the equator. The combination of climate and land means that the agricultural produce is very much the same for all the countries in the region. Coffee and cocoa are grown and exported from most countries. The headwaters of the Amazon's tributaries, particularly in northern Bolivia, flow from swampy areas called the Llanos. These are nowadays used only as low-grade grazing for cattle.

However, up to about 1,000 years ago native people farmed them by building up ridges of soil and maintaining them as raised fields, permanently watered by the ditches formed between the fields.

The main mineral resources are the bauxite deposits along the northern coast, and the oilfields in Lake Maracaibo in Venezuela.

The people

The largest country is Brazil, which was once a Portuguese possession. Most of the other countries were ruled by Spain. The Spanish came to the area in search of gold, and in doing so conquered and destroyed sophisticated local civilizations such as the Inca of Peru. The other colonial powers were Britain, the Netherlands, and France who

owned British Guyana (now Guyana), Dutch Guyana (now Surinam) and French Guiana. French Guiana is the only one still part of an empire. France has retained the colony largely to use as a launch site for European rockets. The position on the equator makes it particularly suitable for this.

Right Tropical rain forest is the natural vegetation of the basin of the Amazon river. The hot climate and the constant rainfall produce a hothouse effect in which plants grow profusely. A continuous canopy of branches and leaves obscures the light and keeps the forest floor in darkness. Lianas and epiphytes grow attached to the branches in order to be close to the sunlight.

KEY FACTS

Official name (Capital)	Area sq miles (km²)	Population	Language	Main exports	Currency
Cooperative Republic of Guyana (1) (Georgetown)	82,978 (214,969)	846,000	English (official), Hindi, Amerindian	bauxite, diamonds, lumber, rice rum, sugar	Guyanese dollar
Department of French Guiana (2) (Cayenne)	35,135 (91,000)	60,000	French	bauxite	franc
Federative Republic of Brazil (3) (Brasilia)	3,285,618 (8,511,965)	153,770,000	Portuguese and many local languages	coffee, cotton, lumber, metal ores, sugar	cruzado
Republic of Bolivia (4) (La Paz)	424,052 (1,098,581)	6,730,000	Spanish, Aymara, Quechua (all official)	coffee, cotton, gas, oil, sugar, tin	boliviano
Republic of Colombia (5) (Bogotá)	440,715 (1,141,748)	32,598,800	Spanish	bananas, cocaine, coffee, cotton, emeralds, meat, oil, skins, sugar	peso
Republic of Ecuador (6) (Quito)	104,479 (270,670)	10,490,000	Spanish (official) Quechua, Jivaroan	balsa wood, bananas, cocoa, coffee, fish, oil, rice, sugar	sucre
Republic of Peru (7) (Lima)	496,216 (1,285,200)	21,904,000	Spanish, Quechua (both official), Aymara	cocoa, coffee, fish, meal, metals, oil, wool	new sol
Republic of Surinam (8) (Paramaribo)	63,343 (163,820)	408,000	Dutch (official), Suranan, English	aluminum, bauxite, lumber, rice	Surinam guilder
Republic of Venezuela (9) (Caracas)	352,162 (912,100)	19,753,000	Spanish (official), local languages	aluminum, coffee, iron ore, lumber, oil	bolivar

ISLANDS
Galapagos islands, Pacific (Ecuador): Farnandina, Floreana, Isabela, Marchena, San Cristóbal, Santa Cruz, Santiago, and 15 others
Area: 3,045 sq miles (7,882km²) Population: 6,000

SOUTHERN SOUTH AMERICA

THE SOUTHERN PORTION of South America narrows gradually towards the south. The plateaus and lowlands to the east of the Andes become less and less extensive until finally they disappear at the mountainous southern tip. The backbone of the Andes continues all the way south, the most coastal of the ranges submerging to form a series of islands parallel to the coastline at about latitude 42°S. At the southern tip of the continent, as the range turns eastward, the whole landmass breaks up into islands, the largest of which is Tierra Del Fuego. This is separated from the mainland by the Straits of Magellan, and at the southern tip lies Cape Horn – two areas feared by sailors because of the uncertain nature of the weather, ocean currents and winds.

The land
The different conditions of this half of the continent are displayed by Chile – a country that is only a few hundred miles wide but 2,610 miles (4,200km) from north to south, from latitude 17°S to 56°S. Its conditions range from the parched

Above The pampas of South America are widely used for grazing cattle. The cattlemen, known as gauchos, are the cowboys of Argentina and Uruguay. Former nomads of mixed native and Spanish descent, their horsemanship made them ideal for tending the herds when ranches were established.

KEY FACTS					
Official name (Capital)	Area sq miles (km²)	Population	Language	Main exports	Currency
Oriental Republic of Uruguay (1) (Montevideo)	68,031 (176,200)	3,002,000	Spanish	leather, meat, wool	nuevo peso
Republic of Argentina (2) (Buenos Aires, to move to Viedma)	1,037,116 (2,780,092)	32,425,000	Spanish (official), English, Italian, German, French	beef, cereals, metals, natural gas, oil, peanuts, tannin, wool	peso
Republic of Chile (3) (Santiago)	292,257 (756,950)	13,000,000	Spanish	copper, iron, nitrates, paper	peso
Republic of Paraguay (4) (Asunción)	178,656 (462,840)	4,660,000	Spanish, (official), but most speak Guarani	cotton, lumber, soya	guarani

ISLANDS
Falkland islands, Atlantic (Britain): East Falkland, West Falkland, about 200 others
Area: 4,699 sq miles (12,170km²)   Population: 2,000
South Georgia, Atlantic (Britain): South Georgia
Area: 1,450 sq miles (3,757km²)   Population: 0
South Sandwich islands, Atlantic (Britain): Candlemas islands, Lekmov island, Montagu island, Saunders island, Visokoi island, Zavodovski island
Area: 130 sq miles (337km²)   Population: 0

Atacama desert to the glaciers above Punta Arenas. The mountains are rich in ores and exploitable minerals, and these are exploited particularly by Chile. The lower-lying lands to the east are grasslands, and so sheep-rearing and cattle-rearing are important in Paraguay, Uruguay, and Argentina. The Pacific Ocean currents sustain shoals of fish such as anchovies and mackerel which form the basis for local fishing industries. The seabirds that feed on the fish produce thick deposits of guano on the offshore islands, and this is exploited for phosphates.

The people
Most of the inhabitants of southern South America are of European descent. All the countries were formerly part of the Spanish Empire, and the Spanish influence is strong everywhere. There are no pure native South Americans left, unlike in the forests of the northern part of the continent. People of mixed Spanish or Portuguese and native ancestry are known as mestizo.

Above The Andes, which sweep down the length of the continent, are volcanic fold mountains, and the highest of them are covered in snow. Gold, silver, tin, tungsten, bismuth, vanadium, copper, and lead are all found in the mountains, but the roughness of the terrain discourages exploitation. The people and animals of the high mountains have enlarged hearts and lungs which have adapted to enable them to survive the reduced air pressure – newcomers suffer from a mountain sickness called *puna* brought on by altitude.

AFRICA

KEY FACTS

Area: 11,620,451 sq miles (30,097,000km²)

Highest point: Mount Kilimanjaro, Tanzania, 19,364ft (5,900m)

Lowest point: Lac Assal, Djibouti 471ft (144m) below sea level

AFRICA IS THE second largest of the continents, being about three times the area of Europe. Three Precambrian shields form the ancient heart of the continent – one occupying the westernmost bulge, in the area of Mauritania, Mali and the Ivory Coast; another stretching across the center from Zaire and Angola to central Tanzania; and the third in the far south underlying most of South Africa and Namibia. Surrounding these shields lie vast areas of very old undisturbed sedimentary rock. The only fold mountains to speak of are the Cape Fold Belt at the very southern tip and the Mauritanides in the far northwestern corner – both of late Paleozoic age – and the Atlas mountains on the western Mediterranean coast, which are Tertiary and formed at the same time as the Alps.

A system of rift valleys runs up the eastern side of the continent, possibly marking a line along which the continent will eventually tear itself apart. This process has reached a later stage in the northeast where the rift valley has developed into the Red Sea. This sea is actually an ocean in embryo, with a spreading ridge up the middle and jigsaw-fit coastlines at either side. That this has happened to the continent at times in the past is evident by the shape of the western coastline, which matches the eastern coastline of South America, and by the pieces of continental crust that have sheared off and lie across the Indian Ocean to the east. These pieces include the island of Madagascar and the submerged Mascarene Plateau on which lie the Seychelles islands.

The climatic and vegetation zones are fairly symmetrical. The equator crosses the middle of the continent and a tropical forest belt, drained by big rivers such as the Zaire and the Niger, lies here. To the north and south, and in the highlands to the east, are the tropical grasslands – the home of the herds of zebra, antelope, and elephant, and the basis of the great wildlife reserves that are so much a part of the modern African culture and tourist industry. In the far north and far south, the continent lies in the tropical desert zone. The Sahara desert spreads right across the widest portion of the continent in the north, and the vast, arid Kalahari lies in the very south.

Africa is the birthplace of humanity. The first people in the continent evolved along the Great Rift Valley from ape-like *Australopithecus* ancestors some two

Above The temples of Karnak on the Nile are a monument of one of the earliest of civilizations – that of ancient Egypt, which flourished from 5000BC onwards.

Right The Sahara desert stretches across the widest part of the continent. It is spreading every year because of overgrazing around the edges.

Left Zebra and wildebeest graze on Kenya's Masai Mara national reserve. Many of Africa's wildlife parks are based on the tropical grasslands.

million years ago. From there they spread out of the continent and populated the world. The continent contains many different native peoples from the Pygmies of the rainforest to the tall Masai of the grasslands. Islamic peoples originating in the Middle East have spread across the northern portion and since the fourteenth century have traded and settled down the east coast. In the eighteenth and nineteenth centuries, Africa was divided among the European empires. France held much of the north of the continent, Belgium the centre, Portugal and Germany the east and west coasts, and Britain the south. By the middle of the twentieth century, practically all of the states had become independent.

Africa has a very high population growth, the number of people has doubled between 1960 and 1990.

NORTH AFRICA

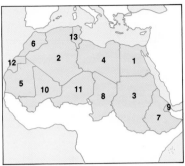

Right The Tuareg, singular Targui, are the desert peoples of North Africa. They are nomadic, roaming the desert with their animal herds, and of the Islamic faith. Their society is matrilineal and feudal, with a class of non-Tuareg serfs. Unlike other Islamic societies, the men are traditionally veiled while the women go bare-faced.

Below The traditional building in North Africa consists of a square mud brick building with a flat roof, possibly supported by arches. Modern architecture may have replaced the traditional mud brick with more up-to-date cements, steels, and plastics, but the flat roof and the arch remain as design features, as here in Tunisia.

NORTH AFRICA IS the broadest part of the continent, stretching 4,000 miles (6,500km) from the Atlantic Ocean on the west to the Indian Ocean on the east. Nearly all of this vast sweep of land lies in the northern tropical desert belt, and is occupied by the Sahara desert. The only river of any importance to the region is the Nile, 4,145 miles (6,670km) long, which rises in east Africa and flows northward through Sudan and Egypt to the Mediterranean sea.

The people

The continuous waters of the Nile have meant that the northeastern corner has been populated and farmed since very early times. The great area of the Sahara desert is sparsely populated, and only then by nomadic peoples supported by herds of sheep or camels. The native peoples of this region belong to three main groups – the Tuareg who are the most numerous, the Arabs whose ancestors came from the Middle East between the seventh and eleventh centuries, and the Negroes who originated in the south and east. In the south, the desert grades into the tropical grasslands. However, such is the pressure for grazing land here that much of the marginal grasslands is deteriorating and the Sahara is spreading southward. This delicate region is called the Sahel and the nations here are among the poorest in the world.

The Mediterranean coast is moist and fertile and so grapes and citrus fruits can be grown. Tourism is becoming an important industry, and deposits of oil and natural gas are being exploited.

KEY FACTS

Official name (Capital)	Area sq miles (km²)	Population	Language	Main exports	Currency
Arab Republic of Egypt (1) (Cairo)	386,990 (1,001,450)	54,799,000	Arab (official), Coptic	cotton, oil	Egyptian pound
Democratic and Popular Republic of Algeria (2) (Algiers)	919,352 (2,381,741)	25,715,000	Arabic (official), Berber, French	iron, natural gas, oil, olive oil, wine	dinar
Democratic Republic of Sudan (3) (Khartoum)	967,489 (2,505,800)	25,164,000	Arabic (official), local languages	cotton, gum arabic, peanuts, sesame seeds, sorghum	Sudanese pound
Great Socialist People's Libyan Arab Jamahiriya (4) (Tripoli)	679,182 (1,759,740)	4,280,000	Arabic	natural gas, oil	Libyan dinar
Islamic Republic of Mauritania (5) (Nouakchott)	397,850 (1,030,700)	2,038,800	French (official), Hasaniya, Arabic	fish, gypsum, iron ore	ouguiya
The Kingdom of Morocco (6) (Rabat)	177,070 (458,730)	26,249,000	Arabic (official) Berber, French, Spanish	dates, figs, fish, phosphates, wood	dirham
People's Democratic Republic of Ethiopia (7) (Addis Ababa)	471,653 (1,221,900)	47,709,000	Amharic (official), Tigrinya, Orominga, Arabic	animal products, coffee, pulses	birr
Republic of Chad (8) (N'djamena)	495,624 (1,284,000)	5,064,000	French, Arabic (both official)	animal products, bauxite, cotton, gold, oil, uranium	CFA franc
Republic of Djibouti (9) (Djibouti)	8,955 (23,200)	337,000	French (official), Somali, Afar, Arabic	none	Djibouti franc
Republic of Mali (10) (Bamako)	478,695 (1,240,142)	9,182,000	French (official), Bambara	cotton, livestock, peanuts	CFA franc
Republic of Niger (11) (Niamey)	457,953 (1,186,408)	7,691,000	French (official), Hausa, Djerma	gum arabic, livestock, tin, peanuts, uranium	CFA franc
Saharan Arab Democratic Republic[1] (12) (La'Youn)	103,011 (266,800)	181,400	Arabic	phosphates	dirham
Tunisian Republic (13) (Tunis)	63,378 (164,150)	8,094,000	Arabic (official), French	chemicals, oil, textiles	dinar

[1]The Western Sahara is only recognized by half the nations of the UN and is claimed by Morocco.

Left The culture of ancient Egypt is held in high regard. The building of the Aswan High Dam (1966-67), meant to regulate the floodwaters of the Nile and aid agriculture, galvanized the world into a massive mission: that of rescuing Ramesses II's Great Temple of Abu Simbel and its neighboring Small Temple, dedicated to the goddess Hathor and to Queen Nofretari. Between 1964 and 1968, with international cooperation, both temples, dating from sometime between 1290 and 1224BC, were dismantled and rebuilt 211ft (65m) higher to avoid the rising waters of the new artificial lake.

WEST AND CENTRAL AFRICA

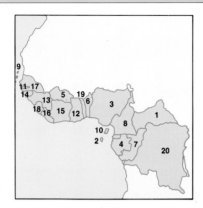

WEST AND CENTRAL Africa lie within the equatorial rain forest belt of the Earth. The natural habitat is rain forest, particularly along the coastal strip. Along the northern shore of the Gulf of Guinea the countries have rain forest, but this changes to grasslands in the interior plateaus. The tropical rains give rise to large rivers like the Niger and the Zaire. The Zaire and its tributaries drain a vast area of the continent's interior and form a forested basin. However, the rain forest is quickly disappearing due to logging and clearance for agriculture.

The people
The range of official languages of the many countries of the region – particularly French, Portuguese, and English – indicate the empires to which they belonged during the colonial period. During early colonial times, the region became a source of slaves, as the pattern of ocean winds and currents meant that they could be transported swiftly and easily from here to the Americas and the Caribbean. The ships then returned to Europe by the Gulf Stream carrying goods produced by the slaves in the New World. After the freeing of the slaves during the first half of the nineteenth century many were returned to the area, and the country of Liberia was founded on this basis. The tribal nature of west and central African societies – originating from the hunter-gatherer way of life in the forests – is shown by the large number of local languages spoken throughout the region; there are over a thousand.

Above Mud ovens are used to bake bread in Ghana.

Right Lagos in Nigeria is a city of mosques and shanties.

Below Hollowed gourds are used as bowls in Nigeria.

KEY FACTS

Official name (Capital)	Area sq miles (km²)	Population	Language	Main exports	Currency
Central African Republic (1) (Bangui)	240,260 (622,436)	2,879,000	French (official), Sangho	coffee, cotton, diamonds, timber, tobacco, uranium	CFA franc
Democratic Republic of Sao Tome and Principe (2) (São Tomé)	386 (1,000)	125,000	Portuguese	cocoa, coffee, copra, palm oil and kernels	dobra
Federal Republic of Nigeria (3) (Lagos)	356,576 (923,773)	118,865,000	English (official), Hausa, Ibo, Yoruba	cocoa, cotton, oil, palm oil, peanuts, rubber, tin	naira
Gabonese Republic (4) (Libreville)	103,319 (267,666)	1,226,000	French (official), Bantu	iron, lumber, manganese, oil, uranium	CFA franc
The People's Democratic Republic of Burkina Faso (5) (Ouagadougou)	105,811 (274,122)	8,941,000	French (official), local languages	animal products, cotton, groundnuts, sesame	CFA franc
People's Republic of Benin (6) (Porto Novo)	43,472 (112,622)	4,840,000	French (official), Fan	cocoa, cotton, oil, palm oil, peanuts	CFA franc
People's Republic of Congo (7) (Brazzaville)	132,012 (342,000)	2,305,000	French (official), local languages	coffee, lumber, petroleum, potash, tobacco	CFA franc
Republic of Cameroon (8) (Yaoundé)	183,638 (475,440)	11,109,000	French, English (both official)	aluminum, bananas, cocoa, coffee, cotton, gold, groundnuts, lumber	CFA franc
Republic of Cape Verde (9) (Praia)	1,557 (4,033)	375,000	Creole dialect of Portuguese	bananas, coffee, fish, salt	Cape Verde escudo
Republic of Equatorial Guinea (10) (Malabo)	10,828 (28,051)	336,000	Spanish (official), pidgin English, Portuguese dialect	bananas, cocoa, coffee, lumber	ekuele, CFA franc
Republic of The Gambia (11) (Banjul)	4,018 (10,402)	820,000	English (official), Mandinka, Fula	fish, groundnuts, palm oil	dalasi
Republic of Ghana (12) (Accra)	91,986 (238,305)	15,310,000	English (official), local languages	bauxite, cocoa, coffee, diamonds, gold, lumber, manganese	cedi
Republic of Guinea (13) (Conakry)	94,901 (245,857)	7,269,000	French (official), local languages	bauxite, coffee, diamonds, palm kernels, rice	syli or franc
Republic of Guinea-Bissau (14) (Bissau)	13,944 (26,125)	929,000	Portuguese (official), Crioulo, local languages	coconuts, fish, lumber, peanuts, rice, salt	peso
Republic of Ivory Coast (15) (Abidjan)	124,471 (322,463)	12,070,000	French (official), local languages	cocoa, coffee, lumber, oil	CFA franc
Republic of Liberia (16) (Monrovia)	42,898 (111,370)	2,644,000	English (official), local languages	cocoa, coffee, diamonds, iron ore, rubber, palm oil	Liberian dollar
Republic of Senegal (17) (Dakar)	75,753 (196,200)	7,740,000	French (official), local languages	cotton, fish, peanuts, phosphates	CFA franc
Republic of Sierra Leone (18) (Freetown)	27,710 (71,740)	4,168,000	English (official), local languages	aluminum, cocoa, coffee, diamonds, ginger, palm kernels, rutile	leone
Republic of Togo (19) (Lomé)	21,930 (56,800)	3,566,000	French (official), local languages	cocoa, coffee, cotton, phosphates	CFA franc
Republic of Zaire (20) (Kinshasa)	905,366 (2,344,900)	35,330,000	French (official), Kiswahili, Lingala	cobalt, coffee, copper, diamonds	zaire

EAST AFRICA

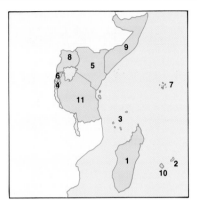

Right A giraffe, feeding from the high branches of a thorn tree, typifies the wildlife of the great reserves of East Africa. As well as being important as conservation areas, the reserves are a fine source of revenue.

Below The Masai are a nomadic people, moving their cattle from area to area as the seasons dictate.

Far right Important fishing grounds lie off the Indian Ocean coast. Local fishermen catch fish with line nets from the coast near Mombasa.

THE WESTERN BOUNDARY of east Africa can be regarded as the Great Rift Valley that seems poised to tear the continent apart at some time in the geological future. In fact, the Great Rift Valley breaks into two branches, the main branch following the boundary of Tanzania, Burundi, Rwanda, and Uganda, and containing Lakes Nyasa and Tanganyika. The eastern branch cuts across Tanzania and Kenya and continues northward through Ethiopia. On the high continental block between lies Lake Victoria, the largest lake in Africa – 26,800 sq miles (69,400 km^2) – and one of the sources of the River Nile.

The high altitude of most of the east African area means that the climate is quite mild for an equatorial region. Indeed, the highest peaks – Mount Kenya and Mount Kilimanjaro – are snow-covered all year round despite being almost on the equator. The natural habitat is tropical grassland and scrub. The great wildlife parks are to be found here, including the Serengeti of Tanzania and the Masai Mara of Kenya.

The people

Most inhabitants of east Africa are subsistence farmers, although only about 12 per cent of the land can be cultivated. Beans, maize, and millet are grown as food crops. Commercial crops are mostly coffee, tea, cotton, and sisal. Industrial areas are clustered along the coast. As in most of the rest of Africa, the national boundaries were drawn for the convenience of colonial powers, rather than on the distribution of the native peoples. As a result, the many ethnic groups are not delineated by nationality. There is a strong Arab influence along the coast derived from centuries of trading to the north.

KEY FACTS					
Official name (Capital)	**Area sq miles (km²)**	**Population**	**Language**	**Main exports**	**Currency**
Democratic Republic of Madagascar (1) (Antananarivo)	226,598 (587,041)	11,802,000	Malagasy (official), French, English	cloves, coffee, vanilla	Malagasy franc
Department of Reunion (2) (French) (St. Denis)	969 (2,510)	565,000	French	rum, sugar	franc
Federal Islamic Republic of Comoros (3) (Moroni)	719 (1,862)	459,000	Arabic (official), Comorian, Makua, French	cloves, cocoa, coffee, copra, sisal, vanilla	CFA franc
Republic of Burundi (4) (Bujumbura)	10,744 (27,834)	5,647,000	French (official), Kirundi, Kiswahili	animal products, coffee, cotton, nickel, tea	Burundi franc
Republic of Kenya (5) (Nairobi)	224,884 (582,600)	25,393,000	Kiswahili (official), English	coffee, fruit, tea	Kenyan shilling
Republic of Rwanda (6) (Kigali)	10,173 (26,338)	7,603,000	French (official), Kinyarwanda, Kiswahili	coffee, pyrethrum, tea, tin, tungsten	franc
Republic of Seychelles (7) (Victoria)	175 (453)	71,000	Creole, English, French (all official)	cinnamon, copra, tourism	Seychelles rupee
Republic of Uganda (8) (Kampala)	91,351 (236,600)	17,593,000	English (official), Kiswahili, Luganda	coffee, copper, cotton, tea	Uganda new shilling
Somali Democratic Republic (9) (Mogadishu)	246,220 (637,700)	8,415,000	Somali, Arabic (both official), Italian, English	animal products, bananas	Somali shilling
State of Mauritius[1] (10) (Port Louis)	720 (1,865)[1]	1,141,900	English (official), French, Creole	sugar, tea	Mauritius rupee
United Republic of Tanzania (11) (Dodoma)	364,865 (945,000)	26,070,000	Kiswahili, English (both official)	cloves, coffee, cotton, sisal, tea, tobacco	Tanzanian shilling

[1]including Rodrigues and other small islands.

117

SOUTHERN AFRICA

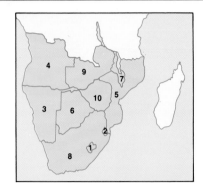

SOUTHERN AFRICA consists mostly of plateaus, higher in the east where they rise to the Drakensberg mountains and the Karoo uplands. The Great Rift Valley has its southern origin in Mozambique.

The northern edge of the ancient metamorphic shield that underlies this whole area is rich in metal ores. As a result, the "copper-belt states" of Zambia and Botswana are important copper-producing

Above Tobacco is an important cash crop for southern Africa. The climate, with its abundant rainfall and lack of frost, is ideal. The large plantations were formerly owned and managed by colonists.

Right The Kariba dam on the border between Zambia and Zimbabwe, about 240 miles (384km) downstream from the Victoria falls, was built in 1955-60. Fisheries have been developed in the lake behind it.

countries. Gold is also found in these areas. Diamonds are formed in ancient volcanic pipes that have brought material up from great depths, and these are worked in South Africa, Namibia, Lesotho, and Swaziland.

This extremity of Africa lies in the southern tropical desert belt, and much of the area is taken up by the Kalahari desert, with the Namib desert along the west coast. The southern tip has a Mediterranean-type climate, giving rise to the fruit-growing industry and the vineyards of South Africa.

The people
The original native people of southern Africa are the hunter-gatherer bushmen. These were displaced about 1,200 years ago by agricultural people who moved southward, and they are now confined to the desert areas of the southwest. As with the rest of Africa, the south was divided into European empires. It is the last part of Africa to be controlled by Europeans. Namibia and Zimbabwe gained independence in the 1980s. South Africa is still under white minority rule.

Above South Africa is one of the world's largest producers of gold.

KEY FACTS					
Official name (Capital)	Area sq miles (km²)	Population	Language	Main exports	Currency
Kingdom of Lesotho (1) (Maseru)	11,717 (30,355)	1,757,000	English (official), Lesotho, Zulu, Xhosa	diamonds, wool	maluti
Kingdom of Swaziland (2) (Mbabane)	6,716 (17,400)	779,000	Swazi, English (both official)	fruit, sugar, wood pulp	lilangeni
Namibia (3) (Windhoek)	318,262 (824,300)	1,372,000	Afrikaans, German, English (all official)	diamonds, uranium	South African rand
People's Republic of Angola (4) (Luanda)	481,226 (1,246,700)	9,733,000	Portuguese (official), local languages	coffee, diamonds, fish, iron ore, oil, palm oil, sisal	kwanza
People's Republic of Mozambique (5) (Maputo)	308,561 (799,380)	14,718,000	Portuguese (official), local languages	copra, cotton, fish, nuts, sugar	metical
Republic of Botswana (6) (Gaborone)	225,000 (582,000)	1,218,000	English (official), Setswana	copper, diamonds, meat, nickel	pula
Republic of Malawi (7) (Lilongwe)	45,560 (118,000)	9,080,000	English, Chichewa (both official)	cotton, peanuts, sugar, tea, tobacco	kwacha
Republic of South Africa (8) (Cape Town, Pretoria, Bloemfontein)	472,148 (1,223,181)	39,550,000	Afrikaans, English (both official), local languages	diamonds, fruit, gold, maize, platinum, sugar	rand
Republic of Zambia (9) (Lusaka)	290,579 (752,600)	8,119,000	English (official), local languages	cobalt, copper, emeralds, tobacco, zinc	kwacha
Republic of Zimbabwe (10) (Harare)	150,695 (390,300)	10,205,000	English (official), Shona, Sindebele	coffee, cotton, gold, silver, tobacco	Zimbabwe dollar

ISLANDS
Ascension, South Atlantic (Britain)
Area: 70 sq miles (180km²) Population: 1,625
Saint Helena, South Atlantic (Britain)
Area: 47 sq miles (122 km²) Population: 5,900
Tristan da Cunha, South Atlantic (Britain): Gough, Inaccessible, Nightingale, Tristan da Cunha
Area: 42 sq miles (1100 km²) Population: 325

ASIA

Area: 17,000,000 sq miles
(44,000,000 km²)

Highest point: Mount Everest,
29,118ft (8,872m), the world's
highest point

Lowest point: Dead Sea, 1,293ft
(394m) below sea level, the world's
lowest point

ASIA IS THE largest of the world's continents, accounting for about a third of the total land surface of the Earth. The scattered islands of the East Indies stretch to just below the Equator, while the northern tip of Siberia lies well within the Arctic Circle. In the west, it is separated from Europe by the Ural mountains (marking the line along which it fused with an ancient European continent 300 million years ago), and in the east it thins to a point at the Bering strait where it is only 53 miles (85km) from North America. In the southwest corner, Africa is only an island because the Suez Canal separates it from Asia.

The basic geological structure is the Angara Shield which lies in the northern central section of the continent, forming the Siberian plain. Younger rocks, forming mountain ranges of various ages, lie around it. From the Angara Shield the land rises as a series of plateaus, the remains of early Paleozoic mountains, that form the Altai mountains, the Tien Shan and the great basin of the Gobi desert. Further south still lie the most modern of the mountains – the Himalayas – the greatest mountain range on Earth. These formed within the last 50 million years as the continent of India jammed into the southern margin of the rest of Asia. The action also crumpled up the rocks to form the loops of islands that make up the East Indies. Along the eastern coast, the Pacific ocean floor is being drawn down beneath the continent, resulting in the island festoons of Japan, the Philippines, the Kurile islands, and the Aleutians – all forming the arc typical of a destructive plate margin.

Like Africa, Asia is beginning to tear itself apart. A system of rift valleys lies across the eastern section. Lake Baikal, the deepest

lake in the world, lies in one of these valleys.

Water flowing south from the Himalayas forms the Indus, the Ganges, the Mekong, and the other great rivers of India and southeast Asia. Those flowing north from the central highlands meander slowly across the Siberian plain to reach the Arctic ocean where they form huge estuaries, such as the Ob, the Yenisei, and the Lena.

As could be expected of such a large continent, all climate and vegetation types are found in Asia. The far south has tropical rain forest. The northern tropical desert

Far Left The Taj Mahal, regarded as one of the world's most beautiful buildings, has an architecture that is typical of the fusion of Hindu and Muslim traditions dominating the culture of southern Asia. A white marble mausoleum for the favourite wife of a Mogul emperor, it was built in the seventeenth century, and now symbolizes India to the world.

Left The snow-capped mountains of the Himalayas are the tallest in the world. They extend from the Indian sites of Kashmir in the west to Assam in the east, and cover parts of Tibet, Nepal, Sikkim and Bhutan. They include two of the world's highest peaks – Mounts Everest and Kinchinjunga. The range is continuous with the other great ranges of southern and central Asia.

Below The vast cold sweep of the Gobi desert stretches some 500 miles (800km) north-south and 1,000 miles (1,600km) east-west in the center of Asia. It lies in Mongolia and China. The grassy fringes are inhabited by nomadic Mongolian tribes and the arid interior is crossed by a road and the Trans-Mongolian railway, which links Beijing in China with the Mongolian capital of Ulan Bator.

belt is only seen in the southwest where it produces the Arabian desert and the deserts of the Middle East. Further east at this latitude the great mountains mean that the desert belt is not continuous. North of the Himalayas lie the cold desert of the Gobi and the cold grasslands of the steppes. Then comes the taiga, the belt of coniferous forest that forms the greatest mass of continuous forest in the world. Beyond this, within the Arctic Circle, tundra conditions prevail. Moist maritime climates lie along the east coast, affecting coastal China and Japan.

SOUTHWEST ASIA

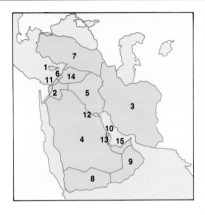

Above right The barren vistas of the Iran-Afghanistan border are typical of the desert landscapes to be found in Southwest Asia.

Right Sheep and other livestock are herded by the nomadic peoples of the region, and are traded at frequent markets, as here in Abu Dhabi.

Below The mosques of Istanbul, with their domes and minarets are a powerful symbol of Islam, the religion that is now dominant in Southwest Asia.

SOUTHWEST ASIA is also known as the Middle East. It consists of the Arabian peninsula and the regions immediately to the north and east. The Red Sea, the Mediterranean, the Black Sea, and the Caspian Sea provide its shorelines, and the Persian Gulf reaches in to the region from the southeast.

Hot deserts dominate the area, with the moister climates confined to the Mediterranean coastline, where citrus fruits, olives and wheat are grown. It was once a more fertile area, the sweep of land from the Mediterranean through the valleys of the Tigris and Euphrates and down to the Persian Gulf was known as the Fertile Crescent. It is here that farming was first known to have been established, and the early civilizations founded.

The people
The vast emptiness of the Arabian Desert – the *Ar-Rab al Khali*, or the Empty Quarter – provides little to support human populations. The traditional inhabitants, the Bedouin, are pastoral nomads. They herd camels, sheep, and horses, keeping them by oases during the dry summer months and migrating to follow the sparse growth of vegetation when the rains come in the fall and winter.

In the early years of the twentieth century, oil was found in the area, and since then most of the world's oil has been supplied from the region of the Persian Gulf. From here it is transported to the industrial countries of Europe and America, traditionally by the Suez Canal. However, fighting between Israel and Egypt in 1967 closed the Suez Canal for a time, which led to the development of supertankers that could carry large quantities of oil around the Cape of Good Hope at the southern tip of Africa.

KEY FACTS					
Official name (Capital)	Area sq miles (km²)	Population	Language	Main exports	Currency
Greek Republic of Cyprus/ Turkish Republic of Northern Cyprus[1] (1) (Nicosia)	3,571 (9,251)	708,000	Greek, Turkish (both official), English	copper, fruit, potatoes, sherry	Cyprus pound, Turkish lira
Hashemite Kingdom of Jordan[3] (2) (Amman)	34,434 (89,206)[3]	3,065,000	Arabic (official), English	chemicals, fruit	Jordanian dinar
Islamic Republic of Iran (3) (Tehran)	636,128 (1,648,000)	51,005,000	Farsi, Kurdish, Turkish, Arabic, English, French	cotton goods, fruit, leather goods, oil	rial
Kingdom of Saudi Arabia (4) (Riyadh)	849,400 (2,200,518)	16,758,000	Arabic	oil, oil products	rial
Republic of Iraq (5) (Baghdad)	167,881 (434,924)	17,610,000	Arabic (official), Kurdish, Assyrian, Armenian	dates, oil, wool	Iraqi dinar
Republic of Lebanon (6) (Beirut)	4,034 (10,452)	3,340,000	Arabic, French (both official), Armenian, English	fruit, industrial products	Lebanese pound
Republic of Turkey (7) (Ankara)	300,965 (779,500)	56,549,000	Turkish (official), Kurdish, Arabic	chromium ore, cotton, fruit, hazelnuts, tobacco	Turkish lira
Republic of Yemen (8) (San'a)	205,367 (531,900)	11,000,000	Arabic	coffee, cotton, grapes	rial
Sultanate of Oman (9) (Muscat)	105,000 (272,000)	1,305,000	Arabic (official), English, Urdu	dates, oil, silverware	Omani rial
State of Bahrain (10) (Manama)	266 (688)	512,000	Arabic (official), Farsi, English, Urdu	aluminium, fish, natural gas, oil	Bahrainian dinar
State of Israel [2] (11) (Jerusalem)	8,029 (20,800)	4,477,000	Hebrew, Arabic (both official), Yiddish, European and Asian languages	armaments, chemicals, electronics, fruit, plastics, textiles	shekel
State of Kuwait (12) (Kuwait)	6,878 (17,819)	2,080,000	Arabic, Kurdish, Farsi	oil	Kuwaiti dinar
State of Qatar (13) (Doha)	4,402 (11,400)	498,000	Arabic (official), English	iron, natural gas, oil, oil products, steel	riyal
Syrian Arabic Republic (14) (Damascus)	71,506 (185,200)	12,471,000	Arabic (official), Kurdish, Armenian	cereals, cotton, oil, phosphates, tobacco	Syrian pound
United Arab Emirates (15) (Abu Dhabi)	32,292 (83,657)	2,250,000	Arabic (official), Farsi, Hindi, Urdu	dates, fish, natural gas, oil	UAE dirham

[1] 37% in the north
[2] not including lands occupied since 1948
[3] a further 2,269 sq miles (5,879km²) of West Bank is disputed with Israel

SOUTHERN AND SOUTHEAST ASIA

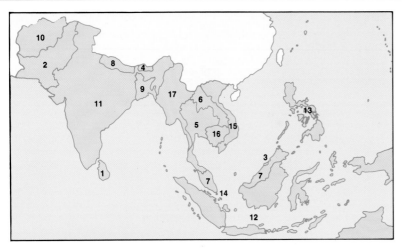

The people

This is the most crowded corner of the globe, carrying about a third of the world's population. The wettest and most low-lying areas are the most densely populated which means that when natural disasters strike, such as floods in Bangladesh and hurricanes in the Philippines, the loss of life is usually very great. The original rain forest is rapidly being cleared by the logging industry and for agriculture. The most prolific food crop is rice, and hilly areas are terraced in order to hold back the water needed for its successful cultivation.

The smallest nation in the region is Singapore which owes its importance and wealth to its position on the shipping routes between east and west. Because of its position as a route center, the people of Southeast Asia are a mixture of Chinese, Malay, Indian, European, and Arab.

SOUTHERN ASIA consists of the Indian subcontinent, and Southeast Asia comprises the peninsulas and islands that form the East Indies. The center of the Indian subcontinent is a dry upland, but the rest of the region is hot and humid with a monsoon climate. Tropical rain forest is the natural vegetation of much of the area.

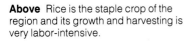

Above Rice is the staple crop of the region and its growth and harvesting is very labor-intensive.

Right The long coastlines and many islands of Southeast Asia mean that there has always been a tradition of trading by sea.

KEY FACTS

Official name (Capital)	Area sq miles (km²)	Population	Language	Main exports	Currency
Democratic Socialist Republic of Sri Lanka (1) (Colombo)	25,328 (65,600)	17,135,000	Sinhala, Tamil (both official), English	coconut products, gemstones, rubber, tea	Sri Lanka rupee
Islamic Republic of Pakistan (2) (Islamabad)	307,295 (796,100)	113,163,000	Urdu, English (both official), Punjabi, Sindhi, Pashto, Baluchi	leather, rice, textiles	Pakistan rupee
The Islamic Sultanate of Brunei (3) (Bandar Seri Begawan)	2,225 (5,765)	372,000	Malay (official), Chinese, English	natural gas, oil	Brunei dol
Kingdom of Bhutan (4) (Thimbu)	17,954 (46,500)	1,566,000	Dzongkha (official), Nepali, English	cement, fruit, lumber, talc	ngultrum
Kingdom of Thailand (5) (Bangkok)	198,180 (513,100)	54,890,000	Thai, Chinese (both official)	rice, rubber, rubies, sapphires, tin	baht
Lao People's Democratic Republic (6) (Vientiane)	91,400 (236,790)	4,024,000	Lao (official), French	coffee, electricity, teak, tin	new kip
Malaysia (7) (Kuala Lumpur)	127,287 (328,759)	17,053,000	Bahasa Malaysia (official), English, Chinese, Indian languages	bauxite, lumber, palm oil, petroleum, pineapples, rubber	ringgit
Nepal (8) (Kathmandu)	56,850 (147,181)	19,158,000	Nepali	jute, lumber, rice	Nepalese rupee
People's Republic of Bangladesh (9) (Dhaka)	55,585 (144,000)	117,980,000	Bangala	jute, tea, textile products	taka
Republic of Afghanistan (10) (Kabul)	251,707 (652,090)	15,590,000	Pushtu	animal products, dried fruit, natural gas	afghani
Republic of India (11) (New Delhi)	1,222,396 (3,166,829)	833,422,000	Many official languages[1], Hindustani	coffee, diamonds, fish, iron ore, leather, tea, textiles	rupee
Republic of Indonesia (12) (Jakarta)	740,905 (1,919,443)	187,726,000	Bahasa Indonesian (official), Javanese	coconuts, coffee, natural gas, oil, palm oil, rubber, tea, tin, tobacco	rupiah
Republic of the Philippines (13) (Manila)	115,800 (300,000)	66,647,000	Filipino, English, Spanish	coconut products, copper, iron, lumber, sugar	peso
Republic of Singapore (14) (Singapore City)	239 (620)	2,703,000	Malay, Chinese, Tamil, English (all official)	electronics, machinery, petroleum products, rubber	Singapore dollar
Socialist Republic of Vietnam (15) (Hanoi)	127,259 (329,600)	64,488,000	Vietnamese (official), French, English, Khmer, Chinese	apatite, coal, iron, rice, rubber	dong
State of Cambodia (16) (Phnom Penh)	69,880 (181,035)	6,993,000	Khmer (official), French	lumber, pepper, rice, rubber	Cambodian riel
Union of Myanmar (17) (Yangon)	261,228 (676,477)	41,279,000	Burmese	jute, rice, rubber, rubies, sapphires, teak	kyat

ISLANDS
Andaman islands, Indian ocean (India): Great Andaman, Little Andaman, and 204 islets
Area: 2,447 sq miles (6,340km²)   Population: 158,000
Nicobar islands, Indian ocean (India): 19 islands
Area: 754 sq miles (1,953km²)   Population: 30,500

EASTERN ASIA

EASTERN ASIA, commonly called the Far East, consists of the desert uplands of the center of the continent, the narrow fertile coastal plains in the east and the island chain of Japan. Most of the agriculture is found along the plains of the great rivers of China – the Huang He and the Chang Jiang. Wheat and rice are the main crops here. The main islands of Japan are mountainous, with only the coastal areas suitable for agriculture.

KEY FACTS

Official name (Capital)	Area sq miles (km²)	Population	Language	Main exports	Currency
Democratic People's Republic of North Korea (1) (Pyongyang)	46,528 (120,538)	23,059,000	Korean	chemicals, coal, copper, iron, textiles	won
Hong Kong (2) (Hong Kong)	413 (1,070)	5,431,000	English, Chinese	electronic goods, plastic products, textiles	Hong Kong dollar
Japan (3) (Tokyo)	145,822 (377,535)	123,778,000	Japanese	chemicals, electronic goods, iron, motor vehicles, ships, steel, textiles	yen
Macau (4) (Macau)	7 (17)	426,000	Portuguese (official), Cantonese	electronics, gambling, textiles, tourism, toys	pataca
Mongolian People's Republic (5) (Ulan Bator)	604,480 (1,565,000)	2,185,000	Khalkha Mongolian (official), Chinese, Russian	animal products, minerals	tugrik
People's Republic of China (6) (Beijing)	3,599,975 (9,596,960)	1,130,065,000	Mandarin (official), Cantonese and other Chinese dialects	animal products, manufactured goods, oil tungsten, tea, textiles	yuan
Republic of China (Taiwan) (7) (Taipei)	13,965 (36,179)	20,454,000	Mandarin (official), Taiwan, Hakka	electonics, plastics, steel, textiles	New Taiwan dollar
Republic of Korea (8) (Seoul)	38,161 (98,799)	43,919,000	Korean	chemicals, electronics, plastics, ships, steel, textiles	won

Far left Hong Kong, an enclave of Kwantung province of China, owes its existence to one of the world's finest natural harbors. It has developed as a financial and trading center. Currently it is a British colony but will be reclaimed by China in 1997.

Left The Chang Jiang river (formerly the Yangtze) is one of the main routes to the interior of the Asian continent. It flows 3,900 miles (6,300km) from Tibet through China to the Yellow sea. Its entire length had never been navigated until 1986.

The people

Civilization in the area dates back more than 3,500 years. The people are of Mongoloid stock, with characteristically sallow skins and heavy eyelids – an original adaptation to the severity of the continental winters. The largest group are the Han who originated on the eastern plains of Manchuria. Anthropologists recognize about 50 others in the region. Most of the other countries in the region have, at one stage or another, passed through European colonial rule. The lingering effects of this are found in the frequent unrest in the area, for example the Vietnam War of 1964-75.

British Hong Kong and Portuguese Macau still exist as colonies. These, however, are to be handed over to China in the latter part of the 1990s.

Japan has a culture all of its own, but part of the Japanese tradition is to absorb and develop other societies' cultures. One of the results of this is the rapid development of Japan as a manufacturing nation since World War II.

PROVINCES OF CHINA		
Province	Area sq miles (km^2)	Capital
Anhui	54,042 (139,970)	Hefei
Beijing Shi	3,386 (8,773)	Beijing
Fujian	47,548 (123,150)	Fuzhou
Gansu	141,550 (366,625)	Lanzhou
Guangdong	89,374 (231,480)	Canton
Guangxi Zhuangzu Zizhiqu	85,133 (220,495)	Nanning
Guizhou	67,204 (174,060)	Guiyang
Hebei	78,198 (202,510)	Shijiazhuang
Heilongjiang	179,069 (463,790)	Harbin
Henan	64,513 (167,090)	Zhengzhou
Hubei	72,430 (187,590)	Wuhan
Hunan	81,301 (210,570)	Changsha
Jiangsu	39,474 (102,240)	Nanjing
Jiangxi	63,654 (164,865)	Nanchang
Jilin	72,228 (187,070)	Changchun
Liaoning	58,322 (151,055)	Shenyang
Nei Monggol Zizhiqu[1]	459,818 (1,190,930)	Huhehaote
Ningxia Huizu	25,650 (66,435)	Yinchuan
Qinghai	278,486 (721,280)	Xining
Shanghai Shi	2,239 (5,800)	Shanghai
Shanxi	60,683 (157,170)	Taiyuan
Shaanxi	75,630 (195,880)	Xi'an
Shandong	59,212 (153,360)	Jinan
Sichuan	219,774 (569,215)	Chengdu
Tianjin Shi	2,395 (6,205)	Tianjin
Xinjiang Weiwuer Zizhiqu	636,075 (1,647,435)	Urumqi
Xizang Zizhiqu[2]	471,841 (1,222,070)	Lasa
Yunnan	168,486 (436,380)	Kunming
Zhejiang	39,317 (101,830)	Hangzhou

[1] Inner Mongolia

[2] Tibet

NORTHERN ASIA

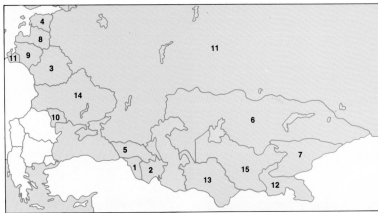

UNTIL 1991, the whole of northern Asia and much of eastern Europe consisted of the Union of Soviet Socialist Republics. As a result of the dissolution of this union the former USSR consists of 15 sovereign republics. Estonia, Latvia and Lithuania are fully independent states. With the exception of Georgia, all the remaining sovereign states are loosely linked through a confederation.

Until its dissolution, the Union of Soviet Socialist Republics was

Right Saint Basil's cathedral in Moscow is a globally recognized symbol of Russian culture.

Far right Fishermen on Lake Baikal catch fish found nowhere else in the world. The lake is so remote and has been in existence for so long that species have been evolving there in total isolation for many millions of years.

Below The taiga is the broadest uninterrupted stretch of forest in the world – a huge expanse of spruce, fir, and pine trees stretching through the sub-polar latitudes across the northern part of Asia. Settlements are scattered throughout the forest but much is still unexplored.

the largest country in the world. It stretched from halfway across Europe in the west to the Bering strait in the east, from well within the Arctic Circle in the north to the hot desert borders with Iran and Afghanistan in the south.

The country
Mountains along the east and south border a vast plain occupied by the grasslands called steppes and the coniferous forest called taiga. Three of the longest rivers in Asia – the Ob (2,120 miles [3,400 km] long); the Yenisey (1,990 miles [3,200 km] long); and the Amur (2,800 miles [4,500 km] long) – flow northward to the Arctic Ocean. Europe's longest river, the Volga (2,330 miles [3,750 km] long), flows to the Caspian sea. These great rivers have been the subject of enormous irrigation projects. In fact so much water has been taken from the rivers that feed the Aral Sea that this inland body of water has been reduced in area by 40 per cent, causing an ecological disaster.

The people
There are about 100 ethnic groups, the largest of which – about 55 per cent of the total – is the Russian. In the European section, most of the rest consist of Estonians, Germans, Latvians, Lithuanians, and Poles. In the Asian section, the Uzbeks are an important group. The remainder include Chukchi, Kazakhs, Tartars, Turkmenians, and Yakuts. The Jewish population represents about one per cent of the total. The smallest ethnic group is the Aleuts, the furthest east, and numbering about 400.

Two-fifths of the population live in the European section, and half of these live within 310 miles (500 km) of Moscow.

KEY FACTS		
Official name	Area sq miles (km²)	Capital
Armenia (1)	11,505 (29,800)	Yerevan
Azerbaijan (2)	33,435 (86,600)	Baku
Belarus (3)	80,155 (207,600)	Minsk
Estonia (4)	17,415 (45,100)	Tallinn
Georgia (5)	26,910 (69,700)	Tbilisi
Kazakhstan (6)	1,049,150 (2,727,300)	Alma-Ata
Kyrgyzstan (7)	76,640 (198,500)	Bishtek
Latvia (8)	24,595 (63,700)	Riga
Lithuania (9)	25,175 (65,200)	Vilnius
Moldova (10)	13,010 (33,700)	Kishinev
The Russian Federation (11)	6,703,235 (17,361,400)	Moscow
Tajikistan (12)	55,250 (143,829)	Dushanbe
Turkmenistan (13)	188,455 488,100)	Ashkhabad
Ukraine (14)	171,815 (455,000)	Kiev
Uzbekistan (15)	172,740 (447,400)	Tashkent

EUROPE

EUROPE IS THE second smallest continent in the world, but it has the most complex physical layout and geological history.

It stretches from the Ural mountains in the east, where it fused with the continent of Asia some 300 million years ago, to the tattered Atlantic shoreline that was wrenched away from the North American landmass about 200 million years ago. The northern section has mountains – the Scottish and Norwegian highlands – that are about 400 million years old, and the southern edge has new fold mountains that are still forming as Africa is thrusting eastwards against it. The movement of Africa has produced the Mediterranean Sea – a temporary feature from a geological point of view – and has twisted the new mountains into a vast S-shape comprising the backbone of Italy, the Alps, and the Carpathians. It also accounts for the shape of the Iberian peninsula, pulled from the gap now occupied by the Bay of Biscay, and the largest Mediterranean islands, Corsica and Sardinia, plucked from the mainland. The Mediterranean sea, with the string of shallow seas stretching eastward ̖ – the Black Sea, the Caspian Sea, and the Aral Sea – can be thought of as the last drying puddles of what was the vast Tethys Ocean that once separated the supercontinent of Gondwana in the south from that of Laurasia in the north.

Left The fjords of Norway are the results of recent Ice Age erosion of 400 million-year-old mountains.

Above Salzburg, between the European plain and the northern foothills of the Alps, is an important route center.

Right Much of Greece consists of islands scattered through the eastern Mediterranean. It is a tectonically active area.

The strains on the European continent have produced rift valleys like those of the Rhône, the Rhine, and that on the continental shelf of the North sea which is associated with the oil deposits there. The great complexity of bays, inlets, islands, and peninsulas found around the coast gives Europe the longest coastline of any continent.

Climates also are complex. The southern section, with its hot dry summers and warm wet westerly winds in winter, gives its name to the Mediterranean climate, that is found elsewhere in the world in similar latitudes in places with similar westerly aspects. The northern areas are within the convergence belt of the warm westerlies and the cold polar easterlies. The climates here are dominated by frontal systems, giving rise to characteristically unstable weather conditions, particularly over the British Isles. The climate along the western coastline is modified by the warm ocean waters brought north by the Gulf Stream. The broad interior in the east of the continent, far from the modifying influence of the sea, has continental climates with very hot summers and very cold winters.

Because of the varied climates and conditions that are present, a wide range of crops can be grown, and Europe is inhabited by a great variety of people. The complex geology has ensured that many different types of mineral resource lie in the area, a fact that has led to the continent's historical lead in industrialization.

The earliest human inhabitants were *Homo erectus*, whose sites have been found in Spain dating from about 300,000 years ago. By the end of the Ice Age, 20,000 years ago, *Homo sapiens* was well established throughout the continent.

SCANDINAVIA

SCANDINAVIA IS THE northernmost part of Europe, consisting of the peninsulas of the north coast and Iceland which is, geologically, half European and half North American. Greenland is included here although it is geologically part of North America. Culturally it is more part of Scandinavia since it only gained its independence from Denmark in 1981.

The land

In the Ice Age, glaciers covered all of Scandinavia and the land is still rising, having been relieved of the great weight of the ice. However, many of the ice-gouged valleys of Norway remain submerged, producing the characteristic coastline of fjords. The Baltic sea, which provides the southern boundary for the region, is gradually shrinking. Each country offers a different landscape – Norway is almost totally mountainous. Denmark is low-lying and agricultural. Finland has forests and lakes and Sweden is a mixture of all these features. Iceland consists of black volcanic deserts and Greenland is almost totally covered by an ice cap.

The people

Most of the people of Scandinavia are descended from the Vikings, an adventurous seafaring people who reached their peak between the eighth and eleventh centuries, and who subsequently influenced the culture of the whole of northern Europe. The original Viking language has survived almost unchanged as Icelandic.

Farming and fishing have traditionally been the chief occupations of Scandinavian people. Nowadays mining and forestry are well-developed and the Scandinavian nations are manufacturing countries.

Left Forestry is an important industry in Finland, since only a small proportion of the land can be cultivated. The economy has always depended on lumber and lumber-based industries.

Below The Inuit, or the Eskimo, of Greenland still exist by hunting and fishing. Sea mammals, such as seals and narwhals, hunted by spear from kayaks, are their main quarry.

Left Stockholm, Sweden's capital since 1436, is built at the edge of the Baltic, where Lake Malar empties out into the sea, and on a number of low islands nearby. The whole city is linked by a number of bridges. It is now an important industrial city and a trade center serving the whole of Sweden.

KEY FACTS					
Official name (Capital)	**Area sq miles (km²)**	**Population**	**Language**	**Main exports**	**Currency**
Greenland (1) (Godthaab)	840,000 (2,175,600)	51,900	Greenlandic	fish	kroner
Kingdom of Denmark (2) (Copenhagen)	16,627 (43,075)	5,134,000	Danish	bacon, car and aircraft parts, chemicals, dairy produce, electrical equipment, fish, textiles	kroner
Kingdom of Norway (3) (Oslo)	125,200 (325,000)	4,214,000	Norwegian (official), Lapp	electronics, fish, iron ore, oil products, sports equipment, wood	krona
Kingdom of Sweden (4) (Stockholm)	173,745 (450,000)	8,407,000	Swedish, Finnish	airplanes, armaments, electonics, engineering products, glass, motor vehicles, oil	krona
Republic of Finland (5) (Helsinki)	130,608 (338,145)	4,990,000	Finnish, Swedish, (both official), Lapp, Russian	ceramics, chemical products, engineering products, furniture, glass, lumber, textiles	markka
Republic of Iceland (6) (Reykjavik)	39,758 (103,000)	251,000	Icelandic	aluminum, diatomite, fish	krona

ISLANDS
Svalbard, Arctic ocean (Norway): Barents island, Edge island, North East Lane, Prince Charles Foreland, Spitzbergen
Area: 23,938 sq miles (62,000km²)   Population: 4,000
Jan Mayen, Arctic ocean (Norway)
Area: 147 sq miles (380 km²)

THE BRITISH ISLES

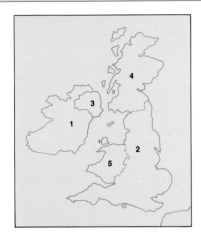

THE BRITISH ISLES form an archipelago off the northwest coast of Europe. At its closest it lies about 20 miles (32km) from the mainland of Europe, separated by the English Channel and Straits of Dover. There are two main islands and about 2,000 smaller ones, including the Isle of Man in the Irish sea and the Channel islands close to the French coast which have some degree of autonomy.

The land

Northern Ireland, Scotland, Wales, and northern and southwestern England consist of uplands which are the remains of mountain systems that formed in Paleozoic times. The remainder of Ireland and England consists of largely undisturbed sedimentary rocks that were deposited later.

Climates are quite mild, being influenced by the Gulf Stream that allows subtropical plants to grow in the northwest corner of Scotland. Weather is very unpredictable, though, being determined by the frontal systems.

The fertile lowlands allow mixed farming and stockbreeding, while large tracts of the uplands are given over to sheep and forestry. The shallow surrounding seas, particularly the North Sea to the east, are traditionally rich fishing grounds, although the fishing industry has declined significantly during the latter part of the twentieth century.

Left The mountains and the lochs, and the distinctive highland cattle, provide the essence of highland Scotland. Scotland is a small country where busy industrial or commercial centers can give way to scenes like this in a few miles.

KEY FACTS					
Official name (Capital)	Area sq miles (km²)	Population	Language	Main exports	Currency
Republic of Ireland (1) (Dublin)	27,146 (70,282)	3,734,000	Irish, English (both official)	animal and dairy products, chemicals, electronics, engineering products, whiskey	punt
United Kingdom of Great Britain and Northern Ireland (London)	94,272 (244,100)	57,121,000	English, Welsh, Gaelic	animal products, cereals, chemicals, electronics, engineering products, gas, oil, oil products, television programs, vegetables	pound sterling

ISLANDS
Isle of Man, Irish sea (United Kingdom)
Area: 220 sq miles (570km²)   Population: 64,000
Channel islands, English Channel (United Kingdom): Alderney, Brechou, Great and Little Sark, Guernsey, Jersey, Jethou, Lihou
Area: 75 sq miles (194km²)   Population: 129,000

THE COUNTRIES OF THE UNITED KINGDOM

Country	Area sq miles (km^2)	Population	Capital
England (2)	50,332 (130,360)	47,536,000	London
Northern Ireland (3)	5,452 (14,121)	1,578,000	Belfast
Scotland (4)	30,412 (78,769)	5,094,000	Edinburgh
Wales (5)	8,018 (20,767)	2,857,000	Cardiff

Left London, with the famous clock tower of the Houses of Parliament, housing the bell known as Big Ben, is the capital of the United Kingdom. It grew as a port at the mouth of the Thames at its lowest bridging point, but it is no longer important for shipping.

Below Harlech Castle in north Wales is one of several built by Edward I of England in the thirteenth century to secure English rule. Since then Wales has been ruled by England. The United Kingdom came into being with the union with Scotland in 1707 and Ireland in 1801

The people

The people of the British Isles are of mixed stock. After the Romans left in the fifth century, the British Isles were settled by a variety of peoples from the rest of Europe. The most significant influx was the result of the Norman Conquest in 1066 when England was taken over by invaders from Normandy, themselves descended from Viking stock. England and Wales united with Scotland in 1707 and then with Ireland in 1801 to become the United Kingdom. The larger part of Ireland broke away to become the Republic of Ireland in 1921.

The British Isles led the Industrial Revolution in the eighteenth century, largely because the mixed geology yielded valuable mineral resources, particularly coal and iron. The United Kingdom owned a large empire across the world until the middle of the twentieth century, the former colonies now forming the British Commonwealth. Immigration from the former colonies, particularly the Indian subcontinent and the West Indies, has added considerably to the ethnic mix of the British.

FRANCE, GERMANY AND BENELUX

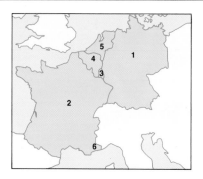

THE AREA OF France, Germany, and the Benelux countries can be considered as a unit incorporating all of mainland western Europe north of the Alps and Pyrenees. The region can be regarded as the North European plain and has the most fertile farmland in Europe. Belgium and the Netherlands, often called the Low Countries, are built up from sediment deposited at the mouth of the Rhine – the longest river in the area 820 miles (1,320km). The Netherlands is a particularly low area, half of it is actually lying below sea level, and much of the farmland has been reclaimed from the North Sea.

The people
The countries of this part of Europe are historically powerful

Right Holland is the area of the Netherlands that lies at or below sea level. The crops of flowers and bulbs for which the Netherlands are famous are grown in the alluvial soil deposited by the Rhine. Much of the area has been reclaimed from the sea and kept dry by means of dykes and constant pumping.

Below The temperate climate and the rich soil of the southern portions of the north European plain provide the ideal conditions for cultivating vines. These are often grown on terraces on south-facing hillslopes in order to catch the sun. France and Germany both have important wine industries.

KEY FACTS					
Official name (Capital)	Area sq miles (km²)	Population	Language	Main exports	Currency
Federal Republic of Germany (1) (Berlin)[1]	137,853 (357,041)	77,600,000	German, Serbian	chemicals, electronics, machine tools, metals, motor vehicles, textiles, wine	Deutschmark
French Republic (2) (Paris)	206,612 (535,265)	55,935,000	French	aircraft, cars, cheese, chemicals, fruit, jewelry, textiles, tourism	franc
Grand Duchy of Luxembourg (3) (Luxembourg)	998 (2,586)	369,000	French (official), Letzeburgesch, German	pharmaceuticals, synthetic textiles	Luxembourg franc
Kingdom of Belgium (4) (Brussels)	11,784 (30,510)	9,895,000	Flemish, Walloon, German (all official)	iron, oil products, steel, textiles	Belgian franc
Kingdom of the Netherlands (5) (Amsterdam)[2]	16,169 (41,863)	14,864,000	Dutch	dairy products, electronics, flower bulbs, oil products, vegetables	guilder
Principality of Monaco (6) (Monaco-Ville)	¾ (1.59)	29,000	French	(tourism and gambling main domestic industries)	French franc

ISLANDS
Corsica, Mediterranean (France)
Area: 3,358 sq miles (8,700km²)   Population: 249,000

[1] The seat of Government is in Bonn
[2] The seat of Government is in The Hague

nations. The fertile lands first became seriously farmed between the eleventh and thirteenth centuries, with the development of such technologies as watermills and ox-drawn ploughs, and a knowledge of seasonal crops. This activity went hand-in-hand with an increase in population and a growth of towns and cities. The famines and plagues, and general recession, that followed in the fourteenth century were early examples of the results of overpopulation and misuse of the land.

France and England were constantly at war, but with the English withdrawal from France in the fifteenth century France emerged as a major world power.

The remainder of northern Europe remained a collection of small states until the early nineteenth century. Only in the 1870s did Germany begin to be the nation that it is today.

Major wars, including the Napoleonic Wars (1803-15), World War I (1914-18), and World War II (1939-45), have meant that the boundaries of the countries of Europe have never been static. The latest change has been the reunification of Germany (from the divided former East Germany and West Germany that had existed since the end of World War II) in 1990.

The countries of northern Europe are now major manufacturing nations, and the checkered history of the region has given rise to many individual local traditions, the basis of important tourist industries.

Right On November 9, 1989 the wall that had divided Berlin into two sections for 28 years, was torn down. This symbolized not only the reunification of the city but also the reunification of Germany as a single nation for the first time since the end of World War II.

CENTRAL EUROPE

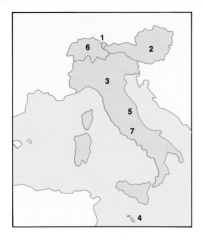

CENTRAL EUROPE is mountainous. Its countries lie in the Alps or in their foothills. At its western end, the Alpine mountain range curves southeastward and forms the Apennine mountains that run down the middle of Italy. The structure then turns westward and can be traced across the Mediterranean by the islands of Sicily and Malta before becoming the Atlas mountains in north Africa.

Central countries

The agriculture of the mountainous areas consists of dairy farming. As the winter snows melt the grass grows rapidly on the upper slopes – the alps from which the mountain range takes its name. Sheep and cattle that have been wintered in the valleys are taken up to these upper pastures for the summer, a way of life known as transhumance.

The mountainous terrain means that it is difficult to transport bulky materials and so the industries of countries like Switzerland consist of very fine work, such as watches or scientific instruments. Since 1815, Switzerland has been a politically neutral country and the stability implied has led to the development of the country as a banking center. The spectacular mountain scenery means that Switzerland and Austria have become tourist countries, with an emphasis on winter sports.

Above The mountains of Switzerland form the basis of a tourist industry founded on winter sports such as skiing.

Left The Brenner pass, with its spectacular roadways, is one of several that cut through the barrier of the Alps.

The Mediterranean peninsula

Italy, being a peninsula in the Mediterranean sea, has a typical Mediterranean climate. The most agricultural area is the Po valley in the far north. In Roman times, Italy was the center of the first great European empire and between the fourteenth and sixteenth centuries it was again important as the center of the Renaissance, an upsurge in the arts and sciences that spread throughout the western world. Modern Italy is an important industrial nation and also has a flourishing tourist industry.

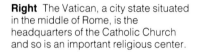

Right The Vatican, a city state situated in the middle of Rome, is the headquarters of the Catholic Church and so is an important religious center.

KEY FACTS					
Official name (Capital)	Area sq miles (km²)	Population	Language	Main exports	Currency
Principality of Liechtenstein (1) (Vaduz)	62 (160)	30,000	German (official), Alemannic	dental products, electronics, postage stamps, processed food	Swiss franc
Republic of Austria (2) (Vienna)	32,393 (83,920)	7,595,000	German	chemicals, lumber, textiles	schilling
Republic of Italy (3) (Rome)	116,332 (301,300)	57,657,000	Italian, German, French, Slovene	chemicals, electrical goods, fruit, iron, leather goods, marble, motor vehicles, steel, sulphur, textiles, wine	lira
Republic of Malta (4) (Valletta)	124 (320)	373,000	Maltese, English	electronics, plastics, textiles, vegetables	Maltese lira
Republic of San Marino (5) (San Marino)	24 (61)	23,000	Italian	ceramics, chemicals, paint, wine	Italian lira
Swiss Confederation (6) (Bern)	15,946 (41,300)	6,628,000	German, French, Italian, Romansch (all official)	chemicals, confectionery, electrical goods, pharmaceuticals, precision instruments	Swiss franc
Vatican City State (7)	109 acres (0.4)	1,000	Latin (official), Italian	–	Vatican City lira, Italian lira

ISLANDS
Sardinia, Mediterranean (Italy)
Area: 9,303 sq miles (24,100km²)   Population: 1,651,000
Sicily, Mediterranean (Italy): Lipari islands, Pantelleria, Sicily, Ustica
Area: 9,920 sq miles (25,700km²)   Population: 5,141,000

IBERIA

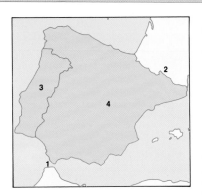

THE IBERIAN PENINSULA is a roughly square-shaped landmass at the southwestern corner of Europe. Over the last 50 million years the movement of the African continent eastwards against Europe has wrenched this continental block from the region of the Bay of Biscay in the north and has rotated it, crumpling up the Pyrenees mountains along the junction with the rest of Europe.

Two main nations, Spain and Portugal, comprise the peninsula. The Pyrenees contains the small country of Andorra, a country with an established reputation for providing fine skiing conditions. The British possession Gibraltar occupies a peninsula near the southern tip – a historically strategic position guarding the entrance to the Mediterranean sea.

The land
The climate is generally dry, the coastal areas having a classic Mediterranean-type climate with warm wet westerly winds in winter. The interior is a high barren plateau with the longest rivers flowing eastwards. About two-fifths of the land area is arable, the remainder being too dry or too hilly. About three-fourths of the arable land is used for cattle, sheep, and pigs. The remainder grows cereals, potatoes, sugar beet, and fruit.

The people
The area was populated 15,000 years ago, as shown by cave paintings in Altamira in northern Spain. Phoenicians established colonies in about 1000BC, followed by Greeks, Carthaginians, and Romans. After the Romans had left, Germanic tribes invaded, and then the Moors in the eighth century AD. The Muslim culture established by the Moors was replaced by a Christian one by the fifteenth century, but the Moorish influence is still seen in Iberian life and architecture. The Basque region that overlaps parts of northern Spain and southwestern France is inhabited by the culturally distinct Basque people who have a strong independence movement. Spain and Portugal have both had a long history of seafaring and exploration. The expeditions of Christopher Columbus were commissioned by Spain in the fifteenth and sixteenth centuries, and Vasco da Gama, the explorer of the same period, was Portuguese. Until the nineteenth and twentieth centuries both nations were major colonial powers with colonies in Latin America and Africa.

The economy is largely agricultural although the warm

Above Lisbon, Portugal's capital and chief port, was wrecked by an earthquake in 1755.

Below The Moorish buildings of Grenada hark back to the time when the Moors ruled Spain.

Right The Algarve is in southern Portugal. Tuna and sardines are caught from small boats.

coastal climates have produced a significant tourist industry.

KEY FACTS

Official name (Capital)	Area sq miles (km²)	Population	Language	Main exports	Currency
Gibraltar (UK) (1) (Gibraltar)	2½ (6.5)	29,000	English (official), Spanish	–	pound sterling
Principality of Andorra (2) (Andorra-la-Vella)	181 (470)	51,400	Catalan (official), Spanish, French	tourism	Spanish peseta, French franc
Republic of Portugal (3) (Lisbon)	35,671 (92,389)	10,528,000	Portuguese	cork, olive oil, pottery, resin, sardines, sherry, textiles, wine	escudo
The Spanish State (4) (Madrid)	194,898 (504,782)	36,623,000	Spanish (official), Catalan, Basque, Galician	ceramics, cork, fruit, iron ore, leather goods, olive oil, sherry, tourism, vegetables, motor vehicles, wine	peseta

ISLANDS

Azores, Atlantic (Portugal): Corvo, Faial, Flores, Graciosa, Pico, Santa Maria, São Jorge, São Miguel, Terceira
Area: 867 sq miles (2,247km²)   Population: 254,000
Balearic islands, Mediterranean (Spain): Formentera, Ibiza, Mallorca, Menorca
Area: 1,930 sq miles (5,000km²)   Population: 755,000
Canary islands, Atlantic (Spain): Fuerteventura, Gomera, Gran Canaria, Heirro, La Palma, Lanzarote, Tenerife
Area: 2,818 sq miles (7,300km²)   Population: 1,615,000
Madeira, Atlantic (Portugal): The main island of Madeira and a few islets
Area: 308 sq miles (796km²)   Population: 269,500

EASTERN EUROPE AND THE BALKANS

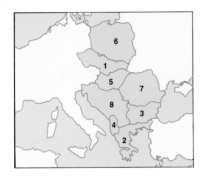

Below Ancient Greece is regarded as the "cradle of civilization." A magnificent society with a distinctive culture flourished there in the first millenium BC, but later the whole area came under foreign domination for centuries. Today, it is largely underdeveloped and suffers from political unrest.

THE EASTERN PART of the European continent is actually occupied by the countries of the former Soviet Union, but the term Eastern Europe is deemed to mean the countries that border these – the countries that, for the second half of the twentieth century, were under the strong influence of the Soviet Union.

In the north of the region, Poland lies mostly on the North European plain. Czechoslovakia and Romania are largely occupied by the Carpathian mountains – an eastward sweep of the Alpine chain – while Yugoslavia (Serbia and Croatia) is occupied by the Dinaric Alps that follow the coast of the Adriatic sea, and Hungary lies in the basin between them.

To the south of Eastern Europe proper lies the region loosely termed the Balkans. This consists basically of Greece and a fragment of Turkey, but also the Eastern European states of Albania, Bulgaria, and Romania. The southern extension of the Eastern European mountains extends out into the Mediterranean here as a series of tattered peninsulas and then the scatter of the Greek islands.

Eastern Europe and the Balkans have always had a history of strife. This is the result of being at the junction between East and West and so being subjected to invasions from all sides. The mountainous nature of the terrain has meant that it was always difficult to establish permanent viable settlements. For

descendants are the modern Aborigines.

Europeans first arrived early in the seventeenth century. The first discovery was by the Dutch. Then came the British who claimed it as a British colony. Until the middle of the nineteenth century, Australia was a penal colony and many modern Australians trace their ancestry from convicts who were transported from Britain. A gold rush in the second half of the nineteenth century led to the exploration and population of the interior.

Nowadays, most people live in the coastal strip to the east of the eastern mountain chains, the Great Dividing range, which includes the New England range, the Blue mountains, and the Australian Alps – with two-thirds living in a handful of cities. The population has doubled since the end of World War II, due to immigration from all over the world. Most inhabitants are of European descent. The indigenous Aborigines make up about one per cent of the population.

STATES OF AUSTRALIA

State	Area sq miles (km²)	Population	Capital
Australian Capital Territory (1)	939 (2,432)	260,700	Canberra
New South Wales (2)	309,350 (801,430)	5,570,000	Sydney
Northern Territory (3)	519,635 (1,346,200)	156,700	Darwin
Queensland (4)	666,620 (1,727,000)	2,649,600	Brisbane
South Australia (5)	379,981 (984,380)	1,388,100	Adelaide
Tasmania (6)	26,375 (68,330)	440,200	Hobart
Victoria (7)	87,955 (227,600)	4,183,500	Melbourne
Western Australia (8)	974,645 (2,525,500)	1,447,000	Perth

ISLANDS
Ashmore and Cartier islands, Indian ocean (Australia): Cartier island, East island, Middle island, West island
Area: 2 sq miles (5km²)   Population: 0
Christmas island, Indian ocean (Australia)
Area: 54 sq miles (140km²)   Population: 2,000
Cocos islands, Indian ocean (Australia): 27 islands
Area: 5½ sq miles (14km²)   Population: 616
Heard island and Macdonald island, Indian ocean (Australia)
Area: 158 sq miles (410km²)   Population: 0
Norfolk island, Pacific ocean (Australia)
Area: 15 sq miles (40km²)   Population: 2,000

Right The Australian Aborigines (singular Aboriginal) are the country's original inhabitants. There is currently a move for the recognition of Aboriginal rights. Their infant mortality is four times the national average and the adult life expectancy is 20 years shorter than for European Australians.

Far right Coral reefs, as here on the Great Barrier Reef off Queensland, Australia, are found throughout the seas of Oceania. The many small islands act as the foundations of these clear, warm-water communities.

147

NEW ZEALAND AND PACIFIC ISLANDS

KEY FACTS

Area: 3,300,000 sq miles
(8,500,000 km²)

In 1957-58, 12 nations signed the Antarctic Treaty declaring Antarctica neutral and reserved for scientific research, and dividing the world south of latitude 60°S into sectors, each administered by a particular nation.

THE SMALL ISLANDS of the Pacific have always been divided into an number of geographic groups. Melanesia was the term used to cover the volcanic island chains from New Guinea to Fiji. Micronesia consisted of a scattering of low-lying coral islands (Kiribati, Nauru, Tuvalu). Polynesia consisted of all the Pacific islands east of 170°E, including the Cook Islands, French Polynesia, Hawaii, Samoa, Tokelau, and Tonga.

The people

About 30,000 years ago the northern part of Melanesia was colonized by hunters from southeast Asia – the same people who first colonized Australia. This is known as the Papuan settlement, or the Pre-Austronesian. The Austronesian wave of settlement began about 3000BC and involved farming people from Asia. In the slow push eastwards they reached Samoa by 1000BC. Easter island was the last to be settled, about AD 750. Europeans explored the Pacific in the eighteenth century, and by 1900 all the islands were in the hands of European powers. The independence movement began with Samoa in 1962 and now nearly all the islands belong to independent states. Half of the population is descended from Europeans.

The first inhabitants of New Zealand were the Maori who reached there from Polynesia about AD 900. The first Europeans landed in 1642. Nowadays, New Zealand's wealth comes from the widespread rearing of cattle and sheep, and industry.

ANTARCTIC TERRITORIES

Signatory	Segment
Argentina	74°W–25°W
Australia	45°E–136°E
Belgium	142°E–160°E
Chile	90°E–53°E
France	136°E–142°E
Japan	no claim
New Zealand	160°E–150°W
Norway	20°W–45°E
South Africa	no claim
United Kingdom	80°W–20°W
USA	no claim
USSR	no claim

OTHER SIGNATORIES, SINCE 1961
Brazil, China, Germany, India, Poland, Uruguay

NATIONS OPPOSED TO THE TREATY
Antigua, Barbuda, Ghana, Malaysia, Tanzania, Tunisia, Zambia

Above A smudge of volcanic ash on the surface of the Antarctic ice sheet in Harmony bay shows the presence of the most southerly volcanoes in the world, making Antarctica a continent of fire and ice.

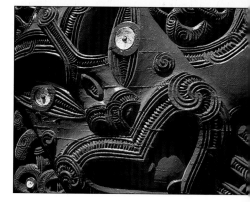

Right The Maori are the original inhabitants of New Zealand. They came from Polynesia about 1,000 years ago, and their culture, shown by their carving, is very similar to that of the Polynesian islands.

KEY FACTS

Official name (Capital)	Area sq miles (km²)	Population	Language	Main exports	Currency
American Samoa (1) (Pago Pago)	77 (200)	34,000	Samoan, English	canned fish, handicrafts	US dollar
Cook Islands (2) (Avarua)	112 (290)	17,000	English (official)	copra, fruit, handicrafts	New Zealand dollar
French Polynesia (3) (Papeete)	1,521 (3,940)	185,000	Tahitian, (official), French	coconut oil, pearls, tourism, vanilla	CFP Franc
Independent State of Western Samoa (4) (Apia)	1,093 (2,830)	169,000	English, Samoan (official)	cocoa, coconut products, fruit juice, tobacco	tala
Kingdom of Tonga (5) (Nuku'alofa)	290 (750)	95,000	Tongan (official), English	bananas, coconut products, water melons	Tongan dollar (pa'anga)
New Caledonia (6) (Nouméa)	7,120 (18,576)	145,300	French (official)	chrome, iron, nickel	CFP franc
New Zealand (7) (Wellington)	103,377 (268,680)	3,397,000	English (official), Maori	animal products, beef, fruit, lamb, light aircraft, lumber	New Zealand dollar
Papua New Guinea (8) (Port Moresby)	178,656 (462,840)	3,613,000	English (official), pidgin English, 715 local languages	coconut products, copper, tea	kina
Republic of Fiji (9) (Suva)	7,087 (18,333)	758,000	English (official), Fijian, Hindi	canned fish, coconut oil, ginger, lumber, sugar	Fiji dollar
Republic of Kiribati (10) (Bairiki)	277 (717)	65,000	English, Gilbertise (official)	copra, fish	Australian dollar
Republic of Nauru (11) (Yaren District)	8 (21)	8,100	Nauruan (official), English	phosphates	Australian dollar
Republic of Vanuatu (12) (Vila)	5,714 (14,800)	149,400	Bislama, English, French, (all official)	coffee, copra, fish, tourism	vatu
Solomon Islands (13) (Honiara)	10,565 (27,600)	314,300	English (official), Melanesian dialects	cocoa, coconut products, fish products, lumber	Solomon Island dollar
South West Pacific State of Tuvalu (14) (Funafuti)	9½ (25)	9,000	Tuvaluan, English	copra, handicrafts, phosphates, stamps	Australian dollar

OTHER ISLANDS
Chatham islands (County of South Island, New Zealand)
Area: 371 sq miles (960km²)   Population: 750
Easter Island (Chile overseas territory)
Area: 64 sq miles (166km²)   Population: 2000
Kerguelen Islands, Pacific ocean (Part of French Southern and Antarctic Territories)
 Area: 2,787 sq miles (7,215km²)   Population: 0
Kermadec Islands, Pacific ocean (New Zealand Dependency)
Area: 12 sq miles (30km²)   Population: 0
Micronesia, Pacific ocean
Area: 270 sq miles (700km²)   Population: 86,000
South Orkney islands, (Part of British Antarctic Territory)
Area: 240 sq miles (620km²)   Population: 0
South Shetland islands, (Part of British Antarctic Territory)
Area: 1785 sq miles (4,622km²)   Population: 0
Tokelau, Pacific ocean (New Zealand overseas territory consisting of Atafu, Fakaofo and Nukunonu atolls)
Area: 4 sq miles (10km²)   Population: 1700

WHO LIVES WHERE?

Above Big cities in the developing world are becoming bigger all the time. Along with the organized development of the city there is always the haphazard development of shantytowns housing people who have drifted in from the outlying countryside to try to make a better living. Often, these shantytowns are built on the city's rubbish heaps where the shanty-dwellers try to make a living by scavenging from the rubbish thrown away by the richer inhabitants.

HUMAN BEINGS REPRESENT the most abundant and successful of the large mammals. Our numbers are growing and we are colonizing every environment. For the forseeable future *Homo sapiens* is not an endangered species.

Human beings evolved in east Africa between two and one million years ago, and from there migrated to all the continents of the globe. They were able to spread via overland routes to most places. At certain stages of the Ice Age there was a land bridge across the Bering strait allowing waves of migration from Asia into North America and hence to South America. The island chain of the East Indies provided the steppingstone route to Australia.

While all this was happening, evolutionary forces continued to work, allowing the development of

physical characteristics suitable for particular conditions.

Nowadays technology and science, rather than evolution, are allowing human beings to adapt to new conditions. Rather than adapt to fit an environment, humans adapt their environment to fit themselves. Centrally-heated or air-conditioned houses allay the discomfort of harsh climates. Taken to an extreme, humans can live at the bottom of the ocean or in interplanetary space, by taking their own living conditions along with them.

Medical science has had an influence too. It was once important for a family to have as many children as possible. Infant mortality was such that few made it to adulthood. Nowadays modern medicine means that children have a greater chance of surviving to adulthood, and the trend in

Right A crowded cityscape is not necessarily a scene of overpopulation. The business quarter of London is not overpopulated since the area can sustain a large population.

Below Delhi, the former capital of India, is a crowded city. Many people move about on cycle-style transport. A few miles outside the city there will be deserted areas, where people have ceased to live in order to move to the city. Although they have few people, these places are scenes of overpopulation since there is no way that any number of people can be supported on the poor land.

developed countries is toward having smaller families. However, the system has become unbalanced and the population is steadily rising.

In AD1000, the world population stood at about 300 million. During the Middle Ages populations were still vulnerable to epidemics. In the fourteenth century, the population of England was halved by the Black Death. However, between 1960 and 1975 world population increased by one billion until in 1978 it had reached 4.2 billion. In 1988, it was up to 4.8 billion. By 2000 it will probably reach 6.1 billion. Development and deployment of resources are not keeping pace and nearly half of the world's population is undernourished, particularly in Africa, South America, and Southeast Asia.

If everyone in the world had the living standard of the average person in North America, the world would only be able to support 500 million people.

Thinly-populated areas have limited resources and difficult living conditions – mountains, high latitudes, deserts, and tropical forests. However, the presence of valuable minerals in such areas may lead to local concentrations of population, for example Andean mining settlements or Alaskan oil communities.

Dense populations lie where soils and climate favor agriculture, where economic minerals are found, or where local conditions encourage manufacturing or trading. In such high density areas individual settlements may merge to form conurbations. Modern farming needs fewer agricultural workers, and so there is a general shift from the land to the cities, often resulting in shantytowns.

HOW HAS THE WORLD CHANGED?

A TYPICAL LANDSCAPE of a few thousand years ago would probably consist of forested river valleys. The same landscape today would be quite different. The trees would be gone and the flat valley floor would be turned to agriculture. A city would be built on the river. The river itself would be straightened to act as a canal, but smaller feeder canals built in the days when water transport was important would have fallen into ruin. The river would be dammed upstream, to produce hydroelectricity, or to form a reservoir to provide drinking water or irrigation. The surrounding hillsides would have changed, too, having been quarried away for building stone, or laid out as terraces for growing rice. High mountains would be turned into ski resorts, with cable cars and hotels. In a politically sensitive area, the landscape might show bomb craters, ruins, and other battlefield scars, and the city could be surrounded by refugee encampments. There is hardly a corner of the globe that has not been altered in some way by the hand of *Homo sapiens*.

The world is divided into different nations – over 160 of them. In most of these, the boundaries were set in historical times, when different social and political conditions prevailed. Even a hundred years ago Africa, for instance, was held by empires that were based in Europe. The continent was divided up into countries for the convenience of the colonial powers. Now that the African nations are independent it is found that each country is inhabited by an uncomfortable mixture of different peoples, and the international boundaries actually cut through land occupied by distinct ethnic groups.

Above The Hoover dam and Lake Mead on the Arizona-Nevada border were built in the 1930s when it was policy to turn any unused land to some human use.

Left The world's largest open cut copper mine cleaves open a mountain in Chile.

3,000 different languages have developed. Religion, too, tends to be more of a dividing influence than a unifying one. Today there are eleven main religions and scores of minor sects.

In well-integrated societies, people who display these different backgrounds may live in harmony with one another, but often they will tend to separate into their own groups. Groups that are particularly disadvantaged, economically or politically, may live in their own separate communities which can develop into ghettoes, and they may then be distrusted by outsiders. Ignorance of other peoples' customs and way of life often breeds suspicion – on a local, national, or even an international scale.

THE UNITED NATIONS was set up in 1945 with the intention of securing international peace, security, and cooperation. Its headquarters are in New York City.

The ethnic differences between peoples cover a wide range of conditions. While the different physical appearances generated through different evolutionary adaptations have given rise to the idea of racial differences, the differences in culture are much greater. Throughout history nearly

UNITED NATIONS INSTITUTIONS	
General Assembly	The decision-making body in which all 159 nations have a vote.
Security Council	Five permanent members – China, France, the United Kingdom, the USA and Russia – and ter others elected for two-year terms, to discuss international disputes and recommend economic or military measures to enforce its decisions.
Economic and Social Council	Fifty-four members are elected for three years. Studies economic, cultural, social, health, and educational matters, making recommendations to the General Assembly.
Trusteeship Council	China, France, the United Kingdom, the USA and Russia, responsible for overseeing UN trust territories.
International Court of Justice	Fifteen independent judges are elected for nine-year terms, to pass judgment on legal issues involving states rather than individuals. Meets in The Hague.

WHAT IS POLLUTION?

WITH THE INCREASES in population, and the increases in technological development and industrialization, there has been a steady increase in the production of waste materials and rubbish. As a result we have a dirty world.

Every industrial process produces waste of one kind or another. If these are liquid, they may be poured into the rivers and the seas. If they are solid, they may be deposited in garbage dumps. If they are gas or smoke particles, they may be allowed to drift away in the atmosphere. At one time none of this mattered very much. Industry was on a small scale and there seemed to be enough water in the seas to dilute any waste beyond harm. Solid waste dumps were small enough to be discreet. Gases pumped into the atmosphere were invisible and caused no worry.

Now, however, the wastes have become so great that they are causing the serious environmental problem called pollution.

Physical pollution

There are many types of physical pollution. Pollution of the land can include the piling up of spoil heaps from mining or quarrying, the spraying of unsuitable chemicals on crops leaving poisonous residues that may lie in the soil for 30 years, and the dumping of ordinary domestic trash, much of which will not decay. Pollution of the water involves the run-off from chemically-treated farmland, the dumping of industrial wastes, spillages of oil from tankers or refineries close to the sea, and raw sewage pumped straight out into rivers. Hazardous wastes may be encased in drums or concrete blocks and dumped in deep water, but these may eventually leak. Pollution of the air is generated by fumes from industrial processes, from car and airplane exhausts, and from domestic heating. Excess water vapor pumped into the atmosphere, as from cooling towers or from rocket exhausts, is regarded as pollution.

Other types of pollution

There are also less obvious types of

Far left Smoke belching out of the chimneys of Port Talbot steelworks in south Wales is a typical source of atmospheric pollution.

Left Discoloration of the sea is an obvious sign of water pollution. In this example, iron oxides from mines in Cornwall, England, are washed out to sea giving a rusty tinge to the sea surface.

Below Intensive industrial activity can produce visual pollution on a grand scale. This view of a copper mine in Utah shows no sign of the nature of the original landscape.

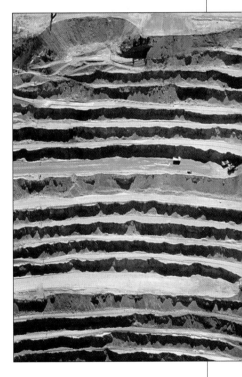

pollution. For example, heat pollution is generated by power station cooling towers, by air-conditioning systems that transfer a building's heat to the outside, and by hot water that is dumped into rivers by industry.

Noise pollution is generated by busy traffic and airports. Disturbing sonic booms are produced by supersonic aircraft.

The intrusion of unsightly buildings and advertising displays is regarded as visual pollution. Excess streetlighting spreading into the sky produces light pollution, which is rapidly becoming a serious concern to astronomers because it impairs their observations.

Large scale effects
Heat pollution on a grand scale has caused the greenhouse effect. Water vapor and carbon dioxide built up in the atmosphere has no effect on the rate at which the sun's rays penetrate to the Earth's surface. However, the re-radiated energy is in the form of infrared waves that

are trapped by the atmospheric gases. As a result the world temperatures are rising.

Then there is the breakdown of the ozone layer caused by certain inert gases such as the chloro-fluorocarbons (CFCs), used in aerosols and in refrigerators, which can circulate in the atmosphere. The result is that more of the sun's ultraviolet radiation is reaching the Earth's surface, so increasing the incidence of skin cancers in the human population.

Sulphur dioxide in the atmosphere from the burning of coal and other industrial processes becomes airborne sulphuric acid, just as carbon dioxide becomes carbonic acid. This falls as acid rain, killing forests and poisoning lakes downwind of industrial areas.

Pollution, a new role
Pollution is increasingly used as a part of modern warfare. Long-lasting radioactive fallout, and the kind of atmospheric pollution that would give rise to a nuclear winter,

are the real dangers posed by nuclear warfare, not the immediate damage caused by atomic explosions.

During the Gulf War of 1991, oil from the oil wells of Kuwait was pumped out into the Persian Gulf and the wells themselves were set on fire as deliberate aggressive acts.

ANY WAY FORWARD?

THE EARTH IS A tough old planet. In past geological times, the surface has gone through far greater changes than humankind could ever inflict. For example, currently there is concern about the increase of carbon dioxide in the atmosphere, for we are living through a time when the atmosphere is particularly poor in carbon dioxide. In the Cambrian period, the carbon dioxide level was about 18 times as great as today's. In the Cretaceous period, it was about five or six times that of today. These high levels were absorbed by the deposition of limestone on the sea beds of the time.

Sulphur dioxide can be blasted into the atmosphere at a far greater rate by a volcano than by any industrial process. Acid rain is one of the effects of a major volcanic eruption. There is even evidence of a natural nuclear explosion from Precambrian rocks of west Africa. What probably happened was that uranium particles washed out of the stream currents until they happened to reach their critical mass and nuclear reactions began.

Perhaps the biggest natural disaster of all was the strike of a meteorite at the end of the Cretaceous period. There is evidence that this happened, and as a result the climates changed enough to kill off a large number of the animal types of the time – including the dinosaurs.

The Earth has survived all of these changes, but animal life only survives them through the processes of evolution. As human beings we would inevitably see any such change as an ecological disaster. There is no possibility of our being able to adapt ourselves quickly enough to cope with these changes within an observable period of a generation or so. Many generations would be needed to adjust our physiology to enable us to survive, that is if evolution still works for us despite our interference with the process. Our big problem is that we are changing our environment at a far greater rate than we can physically adapt to accommodate it.

What to do?

The immediate solutions are logical. Stop population growth. Use only renewable energy sources. Manufacture goods from recyclable materials, and then recycle them when their use is over. Do away with damaging industrial processes.

It is all very well to talk about it. However, we are not machines. Human beings are driven by a variety of motives and emotions. It is our capability of free choice that has set human civilization apart from the blind instinct of animal societies. Sheer logic is not going to change human destiny.

The time may come when general human awareness can encompass the problems of the time, and society and economic systems can develop in such a way that we can all exist comfortably while making as little effect as possible on the natural workings of our planet.

But that is probably some time in the future.

Left Our world is "a beautiful jewel in space," according to lunar astronaut Neil Armstrong, the first person to set foot on another celestial body. From out in space it sparkles blue and white with water and life; the only planet of nine in our solar system to do so. Other planets circle the sun, but these are hot cinders, frozen lumps of rocky ice, or giant nebulous spheres of poisonous gases. The Earth is the only planet to be able to support life, and it has done so for something like 3.5 billion years. Even if humans become extinct, the Earth and life will continue, until the sun runs out of fuel. But that will not be for another 6 billion years.

INDEX

ACKNOWLEDGMENTS

Quarto would like to thank the following for providing photographs, and for permission to reproduce copyright material. While every effort has been made to trace and acknowledge all copyright holders, we would like to apologize should there have been any omissions.

Key: *A*=Above; *B*=Below; *L*=Left; *R*=Right; *M*=Middle

p2:R Beighton/GSF Picture Library. p3: R Parker/GSF Picture Library. p5: GSF Picture Library. p.7: Spacecharts. p.8: Landform Slides. p10: Landform Slides. p13: GSF Picture Library. p14: GSF Picture Library. p15: *A*. GSF Picture Library. *B*. S McNair/GSF Picture Library. p17: GSF Picture Library. p.23: Tony Waltham. p25: Phillips Page/GSF Picture Library. p26: R Macey/GSF Picture Library. p.27: GSF Picture Library. p28 and p29: J Wooldridge/GSF Picture Library. p31 and p32: GSF Picture Library. p33: Landform Slides. p35: GSF Picture Library. p37: Spacecharts. p39 and p41: GSF Picture Library. p43 Spacecharts. p46: P Harris/GSF Picture Library. p49: G Hirons/GSF Picture Library. p50 and p52: GSF Picture Library. p55: W Higgs/GSF Picture Library. p57: *L*. R Teede/GSF Picture Library. *R*. W Hughes/ GSF Picture Library. p60: D Thomson/GSF Picture Library. p63: GSF Picture Library. p65: Jeremy Hoare/Life File. p66: Tony Waltham. p67: *A*. Quarto/Arthur Middleton of Covent Garden. *B*. Jonathan Potter Ltd. p73: Spacecharts. p74: R Parker/GSF Picture Library. p75: David Heath/Life File. p76: *A*. Landform Slides. *B*. Andrew Watson/Life File. p77: T Bryson/GSF Picture Library. p78: GSF Picture Library. p79: *A*. GSF Picture Library. *B*. Emma Lee/Life File. p80: GSF Picture Library. p81: D Wightman/Life File. p82: GSF Picture Library. p83: Ian Booth/ Aurora Travel Photography. p84: Andrew Ward/Life File. p85: Tony Waltham. p86: Landform Slides. p87: W Hughes/GSF Picture Library. p88: Eye Ubiquitous/Trip. p89: Landform Slides. p94: GSF Picture Library. p95: Tony Waltham. p96: Roger Leymoyne/CanadianHighCommission.p97:RoyStyles/Trip.p98:*A*.JeremyDraper/Life File.*B*.R Macey/GSF Picture Library. p100: S A/GSF Picture Library. p101: F Taylor/ GSF Picture Library. p102: Abbie Enock. p103-105: GSF Picture Library. p106: *A*. Andrew Ward/Life File. *B*. S A/GSF Picture Library. p107: GSF Picture Library. p108: Travel Photo International. p109: Andrew Ward/Life File. p110: S McNair/ GSF Picture Library. p111: *L*. Mike Tyler. *R*. R Parker/GSF Picture Library. p112: Landform Slides. p113: R Macey/GSF Picture Library. p114: Juliet Highet/Life File. p116: *A*. S McNair/GSF Picture Library. *B*. M Hirons/GSF Picture Library. p117: S V Norwood/GSF Picture Library. p118: *L*. Sue Davies/Life File. *R*. R Teede/GSF Picture Library. p119: Dave Saunders/Trip. p120: *L*. Terence Waeland/Life File. p120-121: Phillips-Page/GSF Picture Library. p121: Tony Waltham. p122: *A*. GSF Picture Library. *M*. Rob Western/Life File. *B*. GSF Picture Library. p124: *L*. R Singh/GSF Picture Library. *R*. Terence Waeland/Life File. p126: *L*. GSF Picture Library.*R*. Tony Waltham. p128:*L*. Tony Waltham.*R*. Allan Gordon/Life File. p129: Sergei Verein/Life File. p130: *L*. Landform Slides. *R*. GSF Picture Library. p131: Ian Booth/Aurora Travel Photography. p132: F Ralston/Life File. p133: *A*. Landform Slides. *B*. W Higgs/GSF Picture Library. p134: I Gordon/GSF Picture Library. p135: *A*. Ian Booth/Aurora Travel Photography. *B*. Derek Weightman/Life File. p136: *A*. Eye Ubiquitous/Trip. *B*. GSF Picture Library. p137: Eye Ubiquitous/ Trip. p138: *L*. GSF Picture Library. *R*. Jeff Griffin/Life File. p139: R Macey/GSF Picture Library. p140: *A*. Bruce Low. *B*. Sue Davies/Life File. p141: T P Johnson/ Life File. p142: Ian Booth/Aurora Travel Photography. p143: Jan Suttle/Life File. p144: Mike Tyler. p145: *L*. Sue Davies/Life File. *R*. Bruce Low. p146: Mike Tyler. p147: *L*. W Hughes/GSF Picture Library. *R*. Emma Lee/Life File. p148: *A*. P Iverson/GSF Picture Library. *B*. Abbie Enock. p150: GSF Picture Library. p151: *A*. Andrew Ward/Life File. *B*. P Harris/GSF Picture Library. p152-153: GSF Picture Library. p152: *B*. R McGiliveray/Life File. p154: D Hoffman/GSF Picture Library. p155: *L*. GSF Picture Library. *R*. W Hughes/GSF Picture Library. p156: Spacecharts.